A HANDBOOK
OF
INTERACTIVE EXERCISES
FOR GROUPS

Constance A. Barlow
Mount Royal College

Judith A. Blythe

Margaret Edmonds
Professor Emeritus, Mount Royal College

Allyn and Bacon
Boston London Toronto Sydney Tokyo Singapore

ACKNOWLEDGEMENTS

This book could not have been completed without the enthusiastic support of our many students and clients. Their feedback from participation in these interactive exercises has been invaluable.

We are very grateful for Judith Arends' assistance in typing the initial draft of this book and for the excellent work done by Sharon Henderson in editing and preparing the manuscript's successive and final drafts.

We appreciate the artistic talent of Dana Johnston, whose illustrations enhance some of our pages, especially the worksheets and examples.

We also acknowledge the ongoing assistance of Judy Fifer, Series Editor, Social Work and Family Therapy, and the staff at Allyn & Bacon.

Finally, we greatly appreciate the interest and encouragement shown by our colleagues Una Lennan, Vera Goodman, and Carol Gowans; our partners; and our families during the writing of this book.

TABLE OF CONTENTS

Chapter 5: **Teaching Concepts And Developing Skills** 71

Chapter 6 **Values** 87

Chapter 1

Introduction

We have collected the interactive exercises for this book from a variety of sources. Some we learned about at the conferences and workshops we attended. Others have been presented to us on scraps of paper, napkins, or fuzzy photocopies. Still others have grown out of our own experiences with groups. While we have tried to acknowledge as many of the contributors as possible, in several cases, *original* sources are unknown. To those anonymous and creative people, we extend our deep appreciation.

Over the years we have adjusted exercises to meet the specific needs of our target groups, and have informally shared many of our ideas with other group facilitators, therapists and educators. We encourage you to do the same. Freely adapt any of the exercises in this book to fulfill the objectives of your particular groups. Create new ones. Then share your work with other facilitators.

USING THIS BOOK

Have you ever volunteered to give an adult education seminar or run a workshop? Have you been cajoled into chairing a meeting or leading a group? Novice facilitators may recognize the anxiety that accompanies the first encounter with an assembled group. Even the seasoned veterans among you may often wonder how you might inject new life and excitement into a group. The exercises in this book will help you do just that.

Well thought-out group exercises reinforce concepts and help members develop useful skills. Exercises add variety and fun to most settings and, in turn, promote a positive group environment. Developing group members' self-awareness, listening skills, problem-solving skills, personal potential, and insight are but a few of the benefits that can be derived from the creative use of these exercises. Groups with invigorated and interested members can accomplish tasks and realize goals that dreary meetings fail to achieve.

This handbook identifies different group stages and presents easily understood exercises that are suitable for each stage. The exercises can be used in a variety of settings, such as business meetings, adult education seminars, and therapy groups. They may also be adapted and used with various age groups, from children to seniors. You will probably use them most often as catalysts for the work to be done in your groups, but you might also include them to add some levity to your meetings. People like to have some fun, discover something new about themselves, and have a sense of completion or satisfaction at the end of a group session. This book can help you, the group facilitator, provide those experiences for your group members.

PURPOSES OF INTERACTIVE EXERCISES

Interactive exercises, used effectively, can serve many purposes in a group. They can:

- increase the likelihood of active engagement and participation of all members;

- lead to increased cohesiveness based on the interaction and cooperation required to participate in an exercise;

- provide an opportunity for altering group climate (for example, the use of a relaxation exercise can reduce individual tension);

- engage people who may not be comfortable in traditional "talk" settings;

- allow reticent members to reveal otherwise hidden strengths and resources;

- enhance the group climate in a diverse group where the participants do not speak the same language; and

- engage people in the group process in a less formal way (children, for example, through play).

We advise some caution in using interactive exercises. They are not meant to be used as fillers or ends in themselves, but rather as tools for achieving group goals. Some people may find the exercises silly, interpret the activities as play rather than purposeful work, or be embarrassed to participate in them. Some cultural groups view learning as a silent, non-participatory process where the leader is the expert; as a result, these group members may experience discomfort, confusion, and anxiety when invited to participate. In choosing exercises, consider your objectives as well as the diversity in the group, and make sure that the purpose of your exercise is clearly explained.

FACTORS IN CHOOSING EXERCISES

The facilitator must consider the following factors when choosing exercises (Garvin, 1997; Johnson & Johnson, 1997; Zastrow, 1993):

- **How detailed are the instructions?** Examine the age, cultural background, and cognitive developmental level of your group members to determine whether they have the ability to grasp instructions.

- **Who controls the activity?** If the exercise requires the facilitator to exert most of the control and distribute the rewards, this may generate animosity toward or dependency on the facilitator.

- **What level of competency is required for effective performance?** Assess whether the exercise will put certain members at a disadvantage and create power imbalances or subgroups based on the level of expertise required.

- **What level of physical movement is required?** If an exercise requires an advanced level of physical movement, who will be disadvantaged as a consequence? (for example, a blind, physically disabled, or elderly member)

- **What level of interactivity is required?** An exercise that is directed and controlled by the facilitator will naturally limit the interactions among participants.

- **How much time is available?** Leave sufficient time, not only to complete the exercise, but also to make connections to the learning goals prior to and after the exercise. In some situations, extra time may also be required to explore the emotional impact on individual members.

QUESTIONS TO ASK YOURSELF AS YOU CHOOSE AN EXERCISE

- Does this exercise help me to teach the point I wish to make?   yes   no

- Do I understand the steps required to complete the exercise?   yes   no

- Am I able to adapt the exercise to my particular group?   yes   no

- Does the exercise allow all group members to become involved, be creative, make mistakes, find a voice, pass?   yes   no

- Does the exercise suit my style of facilitation?   (Am I comfortable with role modeling, summarizing ideas, and processing material, if necessary?)   yes   no

- Are my directions to participants simple and clear?   yes   no

- Will this fit into my time schedule and still include time to discuss the exercise?   yes   no

- Have I access to adequate space and equipment to conduct the exercise?   yes   no

- Do I have the necessary materials available for the exercise?   yes   no

- Does the exercise fit into my overall plan for my program?   yes   no

ROLE OF THE FACILITATOR

Although your role as group facilitator will be influenced by your group's purpose and stage, as well as by the abilities and ethnicity of its members, fundamentally your task is to guide the development of your group and its members. What follows is a practical guide to the effective application of interactive exercises. A more comprehensive examination of the facilitator's role can be found in current group work publications (Corey & Corey, 1997; Garvin, 1997; Johnson & Johnson, 1997; Reid, 1991; Toseland & Rivas, 1997).

As a facilitator, you must be ever-vigilant, observing individuals as well as both large and small subgroups, making yourself aware of body language, and being generally sensitive to what is happening. For example, group members who begin to fidget and become restless either may be poised to deal with a contentious issue or they may merely need a change of pace or a break. You must listen, observe, encourage, give helpful suggestions, and be ready to intercede.

But, while you may *appear* to function just like a group member, be aware that your facilitation may be compromised by overengagement in the life of the group. For example, your self-disclosure may or may not be appropriate and must be based on its value to the group process. Disclosure based on personal needs of the facilitator becomes self-serving and transforms the group members from learners into an audience. It is very important that you know when to be silent and allow your group to work through problems without interference. In those situations, you can enhance group progress simply by being present.

Your leadership will at times be challenged by one or more group members. Although this can be threatening to facilitators, objectivity must be maintained because competing with group members moves the focus away from the group process. By seeing these challenges as normal processes of testing rather than as personal assaults, you can more effectively deal with the conflict, thereby enhancing the learning of all members.

As a facilitator, you do indeed "put yourself on the line," making yourself vulnerable to criticism and humiliation. On the other hand, you can achieve enormous satisfaction from having contributed to the growth and development of others. When working with groups, what you do is not as important as what you enable others to do. Your feedback should be positive, supportive, and specific.

We know from our experience that it is vital to take the exercises seriously. However, this does not preclude enjoyment and fun, even in the most intense groups, such as bereavement groups. The leader's joy and enthusiasm can generate group connections and commitment, and engender vitality and hope in individuals.

Setting the Atmosphere

Ideally, a facilitator should visit the assigned meeting space, preferably a few days prior to the meeting time, to become familiar with the area and to plan for the needs of the group. A large room, for example, may require dividers or screens to develop a more intimate environment, or an unworkable small room may need to be abandoned for a larger one. Appropriate equipment — chairs, tables, blackboards, audiovisual equipment in good working order, and writing utensils — must be ordered and assembled. We believe that most groups lend themselves well to circular or horseshoe arrangements, although we recognize that this is not always possible.

Consideration should also be given to acoustics. Will everyone in the group be able to hear you and one another adequately? Heat and lighting are important factors too. Is the area too hot or too chilly? Are the lights glaringly bright or so dim that you can barely read? Adequate lighting is required for groups where note taking is required. Soft lights relax; bright lights stimulate. If you do not feel comfortable in the space, chances are that your group members won't either. Any problems with the meeting space must be corrected or modified as quickly as possible.

To create "atmosphere," decorate the meeting space with book displays, pictures, photos, art objects, flowers, plants, lamps, charts, maps, cartoons, quotations written on the blackboard, or other items appropriate to the theme of your group. These should generally be set up before your group assembles. Caution is advised regarding using candles for intimate groups. While candles can create a receptive atmosphere, safety and the possible fears of participants should be considered before deciding to use them.

Music also affects the atmosphere of your space. If you play a tape or CD or even an instrument, ensure that the music is suitable to the age and interests of your group. Background music should relax group members, but not drown out their conversations before the session begins or during breaks.

You should be prepared with answers to any practical questions participants might have about your meeting space — where the washrooms are located, whether there is (or should be) coffee available, and what the rules are governing smoking (and whether these regulations are set by the building or can be decided upon by your group). It is important that you pay attention to these types of details. Not only are they important to set the stage for successful interaction, but they also show your group members that you value them.

Keeping Track of Time

Now that your meeting space has been prepared and your equipment has been checked and found to be in working order, it is time to anticipate the arrival of your first group members. By arriving early, you have the opportunity to greet each member and distribute name tags if appropriate.

Out of respect for group members' personal schedules, start and end every session on time. If members know that you always start on time, they too will be prompt. On the other hand, if they expect you will begin late, they will arrive late, and you will soon find that your sessions begin and end later each time your group convenes. Resist the temptation to run sessions overtime, for you not only shortchange members who have to leave for commitments immediately afterwards, but also invite disruptions as group members prepare for departure.

Break times should be clearly established by the facilitator or by group consensus. Be clear about the length of the breaks and respect the established time frame to avoid being hurried at the end.

As you anticipate how long each activity will take, it is helpful to set up an agenda. This is not an easy task, for each group will approach these exercises differently. For example, a talkative group may need a lot of "air time" while another group may move through the same exercise relatively quickly. Sequence your exercises from easy to more complex and end them on a positive note. *Concluding or debriefing the exercises is essential, for it is at this time that important learning happens.*

Bridging

Bridging is a method that enables participants to move their thoughts from the outside world and focus on the meeting (Samuels & Cole, 1988). Facilitators need to be aware that bridging can easily get out of control and take up all the time allotted for that session. It is therefore advisable to set a time limit for it, either in your mind or in collaboration with the group.

The following outline of bridging techniques can be used for diverse populations either at an initial meeting or for subsequent meetings.

- **Monitoring Progress**

    The facilitator may choose either open-ended questions or scaling questions to monitor progress in a group. An example of an open-ended question is, "How has the previous session impacted your daily life?" A scaling question might be, "On the scale of one to ten, with ten being awesome (great, outstanding) and one being utterly miserable, how has your week been?" (or "How would you rate your progress in this group?" or "How well have you applied what we learned last week?").

- **Question or Comment of the Day**

    Invite members to respond briefly to a question, such as, "What one thing has stood out for you from last week's session?" or "What did you learn?" To a diverse group, you might say, "Tell us one new thing that you learned today, or one thing that perhaps you already knew, but was reinforced today or has a meaning that is different from before." or "Tell us one thing about your culture that would help us to know you better."

- **Homework Review**

    A useful bridge is to review homework assignments. There are a variety of ways to do this, including requesting that members

    ⇒ share excerpts from their journals with the group,

    ⇒ report briefly on the learning derived from their homework, or

    ⇒ exchange with partners written statements about their most significant learning from an assigned reading.

- **Talking Stick**

    Although the origin of this practice is uncertain, aborginals use the talking stick during a gathering to identify the speaker. Whoever holds the talking stick is authorized to speak without interruption until that person has said all he or she needs or wants to say. This allows full development of ideas and encourages others to listen. Everyone eventually gains the opportunity to hold the talking stick (to speak).

    Instead of a stick, another item, such as a shell, a stone, a feather, or a candle, might be used to designate the speaker.

A variation of the talking stick is the ball toss. The person holding the ball speaks and then throws it to another person, who, after talking, then throws it to another group member.

- **Silence**

Using silence at the beginning of a group session is a powerful way of centering the members. Marg attended a workshop where silence was the rule during lunch. This resulted in an energetic afternoon session because the energy ordinarily exerted in conversing with strangers was conserved during the noon break.

- **Meditation**

A guided relaxation practice accompanied by music can serve to gently reengage members.

- **Smudge**

Many cultures utilize the spiritual tradition of burning herbs and/or spices to clear away unwanted energies and promote focusing and healing. In North American aboriginal traditions, plants such as sage, cedar, and sweetgrass are commonly used; whereas, in European traditions, lavender and sandalwood are burned.

- **Bitch or Brag**

Give each group member the opportunity to "bitch" and/or "brag" about something that happened during the past week.

Establishing Ground Rules

Clear and simple ground rules are essential for all groups. As much as possible, facilitators should be sensitive to how cultural beliefs of group members can affect their views of collaborative rule setting and their expectations of a group and its leader. Experiences of oppression, discrimination, and prejudice can have an impact on individual members' abilities and willingness to participate in collaborative goal setting and to adhere to common group rules.

People, whether they are children or adults, tend to respond better if they know the "rules of the game." Some group rules are prescribed and are nonnegotiable. Certain meeting locations, for example, forbid smoking. Another nonnegotiable rule is confidentiality. Personal revelations and group discussions regarding them should remain absolutely confidential and must not be talked about outside the group. Although confidentiality in a group cannot be guaranteed, it is essential that you address this issue, preferably at your group's first meeting. Suggest that if any member doubts whether or not to reveal something, they should not do so. They should wait until trust develops or self-confidence increases. As a group facilitator, be aware that laws governing the reporting of certain kinds of abuse preclude confidentiality.

Other rules can be developed by the groups themselves. Wise facilitators encourage their groups to devise the regulations governing member participation. While this may be difficult for leaders accustomed to maintaining firm control, we find that groups generally devise fair (and sometimes extremely tough) rules for themselves.

The exercise below will help you to engage group members in developing such rules. It has the added benefit of developing an atmosphere of mutuality, safety, and ownership within your group. You will need a flip-chart, overhead projector, or blackboard and at least thirty minutes time for a group of ten. Subdivide a larger group and then reconvene to share the subgroups' decisions and develop a consensus.

As facilitator, you might say, "Think about two rules that you would like to see as working guidelines for the group." Examples might be, "All members have the right to speak without being interrupted." "Be flexible." "Be supportive." When they are finished, ask them to share these rules with the rest of the group while you record them on the flip-chart, overhead projector, or blackboard. When these tasks have been accomplished and the results recorded, lead the group to discuss the rules and develop a consensual model for establishing the ultimate group "working rules." Then lead a discussion on the consequences of non-adherence to the rules and record the agreed-upon consequences. This procedure can also be used for developing an agenda, as well as deciding on program activities or any relevant group tasks.

Reconvening Group Members

After breaks and also when large groups have subdivided and people are involved in intense interactions, group members may become frustrated with your request to refocus their attentions back to the larger group. To ease this transition, prior to dismissing them, have them agree to reconvene when they hear you using a particular gentle noisemaker which makes a distinct sound. You might also contract with your group to use the sound two minutes before a particular interaction is expected to end. Your transition signal might be blowing a whistle, ringing a bell or bells, striking a gong or brass bowl or drum, clapping your hands, or playing music.

TECHNIQUES TO ACCOMPANY INTERACTIVE EXERCISES

Role Plays

- **Purpose of Role Plays**

    Role playing develops confidence in participants and provides them with opportunities for personal development, as well as chances to form closer relationships with other group members. These goals are accomplished by allowing group members to practice new skills in a safe environment before they attempt to fulfill these roles in day-to-day situations.

    More specifically, the function of role playing is threefold (Garvin, 1997; Johnson & Johnson, 1997; Zastrow, 1993):

    ⇒ *Behavioral Rehearsal* enables participants to learn new behavior that can be used outside the group (such as in confronting a colleague, learning assertiveness, practicing interviewing, and resolving conflicts);

    ⇒ *Assessment* determines how an individual in the group might respond in a particular situation (for example, in a job interview); and

    ⇒ *Empathy* helps a group member understand why another person (such as a significant other) might react in a particular way (for example, in a parent-child conflict).

- **Guidelines for Role Plays**

    ⇒ As a facilitator, you must construct the parameters of the interactive experience, first by describing the process, and then by clearly outlining the tasks of the participants.

    ⇒ To minimize the anxiety of role players, elicit their reactions to the roles so that they can work through any negative feelings prior to their "performance."

⇒ Caution participants against exaggerating a situation, as this undermines the constructive process.

⇒ To reassure and encourage potential role players, say, "Be yourselves and act as if you are in the situation described to you. There is no right or wrong way to act here, and you don't have to be particularly talented actors or actresses. Each of you, get into your individual role and let your feelings, attitudes, and behaviors evolve with the part you are playing. You may experience emotions you didn't expect when your role playing began, but don't let that hold you back. The more emotions involved, the more you'll learn."

⇒ Advise observers to make notes on their personal observations and to provide constructive feedback to the actors.

⇒ Critical to the role play is a debriefing process which includes actors and observers. Facilitators must be aware that the actors may feel vulnerable and that support must be available should it be upsetting to some.

⇒ Group members generally report mixed feelings about these interactive experiences. They *hate* the stress of doing the role play, but they *love* the results. So, when you announce that the group will do some role playing, expect to hear some groans. However, when you read the final evaluations from your group, expect members to say they loved this experience and actually wanted more!

⇒ An exercise using role plays is "Simulation for Stimulation," on page 86.

Journals

By documenting personal observations and experiences and allowing opportunities for introspection, journal writing about one's experiences in the group can be a powerful learning tool and an important vehicle for personal development.   Journals range from notes in simple point form to complex personal analyses. They are used to:

- enhance thinking by moving thoughts beyond the vague and elusive to a concrete realm;

> *Starting with self-communication in private you can then develop your ability to communicate with others. Being clear with yourself opens the way for being more clear with others about how you feel and think, enriching relationships and social interactions.*
> (Capucchione, 1979, page 6)

- provide a record of the extent to which members have developed skills or progressed toward achieving their goals; and
- chart areas of personal growth and development.

Your use of journal writing strategy can be directive or non-directive, and can be utilized either at the beginning or end of each group meeting. A non-directive approach applies the techniques of free writing, with the facilitator saying, "For the next five minutes, write down whatever you are thinking. Don't stop writing. If your mind goes blank, continue by writing, 'My mind is blank,' until more complete thoughts emerge."

A more directive approach to journal writing is

- to pose questions and invite group members to respond in writing;
- to ask members to pose their own questions and then write their responses; or
- to invite members to record their ongoing thoughts and observations related to group and individual goals.

Regardless of the approach used, encourage individuals to continue journal writing on a regular basis and stress that its value is based on their own personal assessments as opposed to evaluation by the group.   Reluctant journalists may gain confidence from engaging in the freewriting exercise on page 79. Sharing of journals is optional and depends on the journals' contents and the group's purpose. As facilitator, you can enhance the effectiveness of your group by keeping your own journal and sharing entries where appropriate.

Brainstorming

Brainstorming is a technique used to generate new ideas, share viewpoints, overcome judgmental thinking and single-mindedness, and stimulate creativity. We suggest the following process for brainstorming.

- If the group is large, you may wish to subdivide.
- Give each group a flip-chart sheet and a marker and have a designate selected to write down the ideas on the paper.
- Clearly establish the group task.
- Ask group members to call out short, concise ideas about the topic. These are *all recorded without discussion, judgment, evaluation, or interpretation.*
- Reinforce the point that *all ideas are valued and recorded.*
- Once the "idea well" has been exhausted or the time limit has been reached, have each group prioritize its lists.
- If you have subdivided the group, reconvene and invite each subgroup to present its list to the larger group.
- Summarize the top priorities on a fresh flip-chart sheet, the blackboard, or the overhead projector.
- Now group, discuss, evaluate and interpret the ideas presented.
- Make decisions resulting from the outcome of the discussion.

People find brainstorming useful, not only in formalized groups, but also in families, and for individual problem solving.

CONSIDERATIONS WHEN WORKING WITH DIVERSE GROUPS

Prejudicial attitudes usually emerge at some point in diverse groups (Johnson, Torres, Coleman, & Smith, 1995). These attitudes may take the form of:

- **open expression**, such as name calling;
- **color blindness**, in which the reality of the experience of being different is not acknowledged by the dominant group; and
- **potentially inflammatory statements** arising from unconscious racism, such as "A lot of my friends are Jewish, but . . . ."

A facilitator's "head in the sand" approach to these attitudes expressed by group members will potentially jeopardize the development of trust and cohesion within the group; therefore, it is critical that you address and challenge prejudicial attitudes, even though your action may lead to a highly emotional discussion. Encourage group members to generate alternative belief systems. The variations of the values exercises in Chapter Six provide a useful beginning for examining assumptions and receiving group feedback.

Effective facilitation of diverse groups requires:

- a commitment to attend to diversity issues in the group;
- recognition and assessment of members' personal beliefs and attitudes about minority groups; and
- adherence to Reid's (1991) "Noah's Ark Principle": when establishing a group, attempt to include at least two people of a particular race, gender, or lifestyle.

We hope that you enjoy using the exercises that follow.

Chapter 2

Ice Breakers

Group members often demonstrate some anxiety at initial group sessions. They tend to gravitate toward others who are similar in age, sex, race, or economic status, seeking commonalties based on factors such as their careers, hobbies, or mutual acquaintances, or places where they have lived or vacationed.

Ice breakers serve to bring group members into different configurations, so that their mixing overrides their tendency to subgroup. This enhances communication among a wide range of group members. Besides lowering anxiety and changing configurations, ice breakers also provide opportunities for interaction, the first step to accomplishing the group's objectives. As facilitator, you must keep these objectives in mind when choosing ice breakers for your particular group. If, for example, your group is a therapy or psychoeducational group which leans toward the emotional, you would select a different ice breaker than if your group were task-oriented.

Choose your ice breakers wisely. In fact, it is critical that you be aware of the impact of ice breakers on the spirit of your group. Choosing an appropriate ice breaker can leave group members excited, open, and optimistic; whereas, using an inappropriate one may leave them feeling apprehensive and threatened.

SHORT DIVISION:
MANAGING LARGE GROUPS
BY SUBDIVIDING

Because a large group is often daunting, even overwhelming, to group members (and the facilitator too), your subdividing it into more manageable smaller groups will increase group members' comfort and participation levels. The following series of exercises are methods of dividing large groups into smaller ones.

The Numbers Game

This exercise is best illustrated by example. If you have forty people in a large group and your goal is to establish four smaller groups, direct individual members to call out the number, "One," "Two," "Three," or "Four" in a series. Repeat this process around the room until everyone has called out a number between one and four.

Then instruct the "Ones" to gather with other "Ones," "Twos" with "Twos," and so on to form groups. You will then have established four groups of ten. If, of course, you want ten groups of four, your group must number itself from one to ten, following which all the "Ones," "Twos," etc. form groups. To avoid confusion, have the groups stand in different locations in the room, the "Ones" in one corner, the "Twos" in another, and so on. Group sizes may not always be equal, and "leftover" members can be asked to join one of the groups or form their own group.

For variation, "A," "B," and "C" can be used as a dividing strategy.

When Were You Born?

Divide participants into groups according to their birth months. For example, all people with January birthdays would comprise one group. (It's amazing how often this results in evenly distributed groups.)

People can also be divided into groups based on the season in which they were born or on their astrological sign (i.e., Taurus, Aquarius, Capricorn).

What Shape Are You In?

Cut various shapes out of paper or light cardboard. These may be animal shapes, geometrical shapes, or seasonal shapes (pumpkins, witches, ghosts, Santas, Christmas trees). Be creative — we have used perogie, cabbage roll, and sausage shapes to represent Ukrainian food. The variety of shapes you use corresponds to how many groups you want, and the quantity of a particular shape represents how many members you want in each group. For example, if you want five groups, cut out five different animals, and if you want four members in each group, cut out four cats, four elephants, four squirrels, etc.

Place the shapes in a container and invite members to select one shape. They then locate their groups by matching the shapes they have drawn.

Action Animals

Write the names of animals on slips of paper, place the slips in a container, and invite members to choose one piece of paper, but keep what they have drawn secret.

Then instruct participants not to speak, but to find fellow

animal group members by acting out or making the sound of the animal each has picked.

INTRODUCTIONS: LEARNING ABOUT GROUP MEMBERS

OBJECTIVE:
- To help people become acquainted with other group members.

MATERIALS:
- No special materials

TIME REQUIRED:
- Three minutes per member

GROUP SIZE:
- Any number

PROCESS:
- Say, "Choose a partner. Each of you, take a turn in briefly speaking to your partner about yourself. Talk about who you are, what you do, or where you work or attend school. Your partner will then introduce you to the group, telling us about you."

- After these introductions, you may want participants to reflect on their behavior in groups. In that case, pose such questions as:
    ⇒ Who took the initiative in choosing a partner?
    ⇒ Who tended to wait for others to choose them?
    ⇒ What have you learned about your initial behavior in groups?
    ⇒ How might this affect your functioning in this group?

VARIATIONS:
- Invite participants to talk about something they are personally proud of.
- Ask participants to talk about something in their culture that they appreciate.

FACILITATORS' NOTES / TIPS:
- This exercise is probably the most common method of getting to know one another in a group.
- For some, choosing a partner can be a stressful experience, as members may fear not being chosen or may be too embarrassed to choose someone for fear of rejection. Use your discretion and arrange partnerships if you assess that choosing may lead to anxiety.

WHO'S DONE IT?
MEETING OTHER MEMBERS

OBJECTIVE:
- Because group members initially gravitate toward others they view as similar to themselves, this ice breaker allows even the most reticent members to meet others in an informal, game-like atmosphere. If some members are already acquainted with one another, this may also help them to see their fellow participants in new ways.

MATERIALS:
- "Who's Done It?" handout for each participant – this handout contains questions such as, Who has . . .

  ⇒ jumped out of a plane with a parachute?
  ⇒ scuba-dived?
  ⇒ become a chocoholic?
  ⇒ milked a cow?
  ⇒ played a stringed instrument?
  ⇒ never been married?
  ⇒ had more than four children?
  ⇒ had more than four pets (at one time)?
  ⇒ owned a motorcycle?
  ⇒ crossed the equator?
  ⇒ baked bread?
  ⇒ played basketball?
  ⇒ gone camping?
  ⇒ been tattooed?

  Beside each question is space for a signature.
- Pen or pencil for each person

TIME REQUIRED:
- Fifteen minutes

GROUP SIZE:
- Unlimited

PROCESS:
- Say, "You have fifteen minutes to complete this exercise. Circulate around the room and ask individual group members to sign their names beside *one* of the questions to which they can truthfully answer, 'Yes.' You must have a different person sign each question; one person may not sign more than one question on a particular sheet."

VARIATIONS:

- Your handout might also be arranged like a bingo card, with the questions and signature spaces occupying the squares. The first person to get a blackout shouts "Bingo!" or, if time is short, the first to fill a designated number of columns or rows calls out "Bingo!" You may choose to award a prize to the winner. (See page 27 for a sample Ice Breaker Bingo card.)

- Adapt this exercise for different sizes and types of groups – and use it at conferences, workshops, and social events. It's a great mixer while guests are arriving for a potluck social occasion.

- Using pictures or symbols along with your specially tailored questions (such as, "Who's ridden a bicycle last week? gone swimming last summer? visited their grandparent this year?") enables you to use it with young children.

**FACILITATORS'
NOTES / TIPS**

- Be sure to develop questions which are *appropriately* matched to your group.

***YOUR* NOTES:**

ICE BREAKER BINGO

FIND SOMEONE WHO FITS EACH DESCRIPTION. WRITE HIS/HER NAME IN THE BLANK SPACE.

Someone who's grown up in the country Name:	Someone who's crossed the equator Name:	Someone who's had more than four pets (at one time) Name:	Someone who's played basketball Name:	Someone who's gone camping Name:
Someone who's jumped out of a plane Name:	Someone who loves curry Name:	Someone who does *not* have pierced ears Name:	Someone who eats rice daily Name:	Someone who has a purple jacket Name:
Someone who's played a stringed instrument Name:	Someone who was born in another country Name:	**FREE xxxxx FREE** Someone who's Me! Name: **FREE xxxxx FREE**	Someone who's had more than four children Name:	Someone who's growing African violets Name:
Someone who's never been married Name:	Someone who's a chocoholic Name:	Someone who's ridden on a motorcycle Name:	Someone who's played in a band Name:	Someone who's milked a cow Name:
Someone who's *made* perogies Name:	Someone who's attended live theater Name:	Someone who's scuba dived Name:	Someone who bakes bread regularly Name:	Someone who's been tattooed Name:

GETTING ACQUAINTED: SETTING A COMFORTABLE CLIMATE

OBJECTIVE:

- By participating in this in-depth exercise, group members come to know one another better and may therefore feel more comfortable in the group.

MATERIALS:

- A list of fill-in-the-blank statements for each participant – choose from the following or create your own:
    - ⇒ My name is _____.
    - ⇒ My birthplace is _____.
    - ⇒ Something I enjoy doing is _____.
    - ⇒ When I feel nervous in a new situation, I usually _____.
    - ⇒ My reason for attending this session is _____.
    - ⇒ Something I can't part with is _____.
    - ⇒ My favorite television show is _____.
    - ⇒ My favorite snack is _____.
    - ⇒ My favorite animal is _____ because _____.
    - ⇒ My favorite person is _____ because _____.
    - ⇒ Someone who has made me feel good recently is _____ because _____.
    - ⇒ The best (or worst) time of my day is _____ because _____.

  The statements above are designed primarily for new groups, as they are generally non-threatening. For established groups, choose statements with more substance. You might also use other sentences that are more relevant to your particular group's interests and objectives.
  So that this activity does not occupy too much time, limit your list to four or five statements.
- Pen or pencil for each person

TIME REQUIRED:

- Ten to fifteen minutes

GROUP SIZE:

- Any size; large groups may be subdivided.

PROCESS:
- Say, "I'd like you to respond in writing to the statements listed on your handout. Then find a partner and share your responses with him or her. Don't be too long-winded or spend a lot of time with just one person. Rather, circulate and try to meet as many new people as you can. If you have time, you may return to earlier partners and explore your answers more fully."

VARIATION:
- Use one or two of the questions at the beginning of each group session.

FACILITATORS' NOTES / TIPS:
- At some point you might draw the group's attention to the increased noise level in the room – which indicates group members' increased comfort level with one another.

YOUR NOTES:

THE ROUND: RECALLING NAMES

OBJECTIVE:	• Group members feel more comfortable when they have learned one another's names. This exercise enables people to become acquainted by recalling participants' names.
MATERIALS:	• No special materials
TIME REQUIRED:	• Ten minutes
GROUP SIZE:	• Up to ten or twelve members
PROCESS:	• Say (indicating where to start), "Starting here, please state your first [or full] name. Then the person next to you will call out his or her name, as well as your name. The exercise continues until everyone has given the names of all the preceding members in addition to his or her own. To make this easier and more fun, you may help the person whose task it is to name."
VARIATIONS:	• In a small group, invite members to create a seating plan showing the name and location of each person.
	• Draw the seating plan of a large group on a flip-chart or blackboard that is visible to all members.
	• On a flip-chart or blackboard, create a skeleton seating plan and then invite members to come forward one at a time to write their names and draw pictures or symbols representing their names in the appropriate locations.
FACILITATORS' NOTES / TIPS	• Because a person's name is so important, ensure that you have large, easy-to-read name tags or place cards available to use.
	• Repeating name exercises during subsequent meetings helps to reinforce the learning of names. Knowing the names of group members is essential for engaging them in activities.
	• We suggest that even members of large groups should state their names, though the likelihood of people remembering them all is slim. People generally enjoy stating their names, and feel acknowledged when they are asked to do so.

THE GAME OF THE NAME:
RECALLING NAMES

OBJECTIVE:
- This exercise can be used as an ice breaker in children's groups, or simply as an occasion for group members to relax and have fun after they have met a few times. As an added bonus, it reinforces members learning one another's names.

MATERIALS:
- No special materials

TIME REQUIRED:
- Ten or fifteen minutes at the beginning of a session

GROUP SIZE:
- Best in groups of no more than twenty

PROCESS:
- Say, "Let's form a circle. I will begin by giving my first name and then the name of a fruit or vegetable whose first letter matches the first letter of my name. For example, I'm Mary Mango.
"Moving clockwise, the person beside me will give his or her first name and the name of a fruit or vegetable that hasn't already been mentioned; then he or she will repeat my name and the fruit I mentioned. 'I am Betty Broccoli and this is Mary Mango.'
"The game continues around the circle until all members have added their names and ingredients to the 'salad' and have repeated those that preceded them."

- The game can end here, or it can continue with members taking their turns in reverse order so that each member will eventually have a chance to repeat all the other names. As the game becomes more complex, encourage group members to assist one another in recalling their names and ingredients.

VARIATIONS:
- To make the game even more challenging, ask participants to choose any fruit or vegetable, not necessarily one that matches their names' first letters.
- Invite members to state their names and relate them to your group theme or topic of discussion. For

example, in a chemistry class, someone might be Carol Carbon; in a camping group, a member might be Harry Hamburger or Annie Ant.

- In diverse groups, members might be invited to link their names with significant words in their cultural or social groups.
- Ask players to state their name and nickname.

FACILITATORS' NOTES / TIPS

- Learning people's names requires time and practice. You can help group members learn them by frequently addressing individuals by name throughout the session.

***YOUR* NOTES:**

WHAT'S IN YOUR NAME?: TALKING ABOUT YOUR NAME

OBJECTIVE:
- Used either shortly after a group forms or after it has met several times, this exercise helps members to recall one another's names and may lead to introspection about their own names.

MATERIALS:
- No special materials

TIME REQUIRED:
- One minute per group member

GROUP SIZE:
- Up to twenty members

PROCESS:
- Say, "Most people, when they introduce themselves, have unique ways of describing their names." Give an example. (Judith, for instance, would say, "My name is Judith Blythe – *Blythe* like the spirit, only with a *y*.") Then say, "Please state your full name and describe something about it. Your brief description will help the rest of us to remember your name."

VARIATIONS:
- Members state their names and briefly describe how they feel about them.
- Members explain how they were given their names.
- Members state their names and then state the names they wish they had been given and why.

FACILITATORS' NOTES / TIPS
- Showing respect and positive regard for people begins with knowing and using their names correctly. Therefore, accurate pronunciation of foreign names, although sometimes challenging, is very important.

YOUR NOTES:

THE BAGGAGE DEPARTMENT: SHOWING AND TELLING

OBJECTIVE:
- In our pockets or purses we carry items that are important to us. Group members can use these items to introduce themselves.

MATERIALS:
- Anything participants have in pockets, purses, wallets or briefcases – lipsticks, combs, pictures, notebooks, etc.

TIME REQUIRED:
- From a few minutes to a half hour, depending on the size and purpose of the group

GROUP SIZE:
- Best in smaller groups

PROCESS:
- Say, "As a way of introducing yourself to the group, choose something you have in your wallet, pocket, or purse and explain why it is meaningful to you or how it represents you."

VARIATIONS:
- Invite members to bring for "show and tell" at a subsequent session, a symbol that relates to the topic being discussed in the group.
- Request members to bring for "show and tell" an object that has special meaning for them.
- Suggest that members each bring a special gift they have received, and be prepared to tell the group about its personal significance.
- Ask each member to bring a picture from a magazine that is personally meaningful, and explain why.
- Request that they each bring an object or symbol that has meaning in their particular culture.
- Direct group members to answer simple questions, such as, "What is your favorite food? television program? author?" or "What is your most memorable vacation? holiday season?" or "Whom do you particularly admire?" Members should be prepared to explain their choices.

FACILITATORS' NOTES / TIPS
- This exercise, with its variations, can serve as a beginning ritual for each group session.

I'LL TELL YOU IF YOU'LL TELL ME: ROLE MODELING AND RISK TAKING

OBJECTIVE:
- This exercise provides the opportunity for a mutual exchange between you and group members. As you provide far more answers than each group member, you are taking the greater risk, thereby acting as role model for those in the group.

MATERIALS:
- No special materials

TIME REQUIRED:
- Ten to twenty minutes, depending on the size of the group

GROUP SIZE:
- No more than twenty members

PROCESS:
- Say, "In a round robin fashion, I'd like you to share something about yourself. Then you may ask one question of me. This process continues until all of you have shared and asked me a question. As I'm more on the 'hot seat' than you are, I reserve the right to pass if I am uncomfortable with the question."

FACILITATORS' NOTES / TIPS
- We have found this exercise a useful way of exchanging information in that it gives group members an opportunity to get to know the facilitator.
- If you are uncertain how you should introduce yourself to your group, this exercise will eliminate that concern. Group members will ask you what they need to know.

YOUR NOTES:

THE FIRST BLUSH: EXPLORING FIRST IMPRESSIONS

OBJECTIVE:
- This lighthearted exercise is a good method of introducing members to one another. It also increases the participants' awareness of others and provides them with an opportunity to share information about themselves with the group.

MATERIALS:
- No special materials

TIME REQUIRED:
- Five minutes per participant

GROUP SIZE:
- Best in groups with fewer than fifteen members

PROCESS:
- Say, "Turn to the person on your right and ask only his or her name. While you are doing that, notice anything about that person that is *positive*. I'll give you about a minute to do that. Then I'll ask you to describe to the rest of the group what you saw in your first impression. The named individual will have an opportunity to comment on your impression."

VARIATION:
- A discussion of first impressions, how valid they are, and how they may be confusing or misleading is a natural outcome of this exercise.

FACILITATORS' NOTES / TIPS
- As this exercise may be a threatening experience for some, make sure that you emphasize that all observations must be positive.

YOUR NOTES:

SINGING IN THE RAIN: TAKING RISKS

OBJECTIVE:
- This energy-enhancing exercise is designed to help people take risks, with the idea that if you can sing in a group, you can do anything.

MATERIALS:
- No special materials.

TIME REQUIRED:
- Two minutes per group member

GROUP SIZE:
- No more than twenty members

PROCESS:
- Say, "Take one minute to think of a familiar song. This shouldn't be just any song, but rather one you will feel comfortable singing in this group. After the minute is up, I'll ask each of you in turn to sing three or four lines of the song you've chosen. I reserve the right to stop any 'hams' who might sing for too long."

VARIATION:
- Instead of singing, group members may be asked to tell a joke, recite a poem or nursery rhyme, or impersonate a character.

FACILITATORS' NOTES / TIPS
- Although certain people proclaim to hate this exercise, it tends to draw people together. In cultures where singing is common, this exercise is very popular.

YOUR NOTES:

Chapter 3

Enhancing Group Functioning

Poor leadership skills and negative group chemistry can threaten group productivity. Even with a consistent agenda, no two groups are the same in their verbal and nonverbal communication, listening skills, member self-concepts, interpersonal relationships, and group goals – all of which contribute to a group's functioning.

Chapter Three offers exercises that help members to become conscious of their own behaviors in groups, gain awareness of the behaviors of other group members, develop trust, and confront conflict. Your ultimate goal as group facilitator is twofold: to enhance the worth and dignity of each participant as he or she works through the group's tasks, and to encourage group cohesiveness in accomplishing individual and group goals.

LET'S GET TOGETHER:
BUILDING COHESIVENESS

OBJECTIVE:
- To help build group rapport and cohesiveness.

MATERIALS:
- A sheet of paper and one pen per working group

TIME REQUIRED:
- Fifteen to thirty minutes

GROUP SIZE:
- Three to ten people; subdivide larger groups

PROCESS:
- Say, "Create a name for your particular group. Then develop a logo [coat of arms, bumper sticker] that represents your purpose for meeting, your personalities, and/or your cultural heritage. Finally, plan and prepare this creation for presentation to the larger group. Remember that all members should be involved in this process."

VARIATION:
- Ask each group to prepare a song, short story, or poem that reflects the theme to be discussed that day.

FACILITATORS' NOTES / TIPS
- Use this exercise with people of diverse ages and cultural backgrounds in order to develop a sense of belonging and connectedness. It is also effective:
  ⇒ with newly formed groups;
  ⇒ in cabin or camp situations;
  ⇒ at workshops or in environments where new learning projects are being introduced; and
  ⇒ in social situations (e.g., a wedding, where the bride and groom kiss only after a group or table of guests performs a song, poem, etc. about love and marriage).

YOUR NOTES:

ELEPHANT IN THE MEETING ROOM: DEALING WITH ROAD BLOCKS

Adapted from an exercise by M.H. Typpo and J.M. Hastings (1984)

OBJECTIVE:	• Concerns or conflicts may sometimes arise within a group. This exercise allows these concerns to be identified and provides members with the opportunity to discuss them.
MATERIALS:	• The story, "The Large Gray Elephant"
TIME REQUIRED:	• One hour
GROUP SIZE:	• Ten
PROCESS:	• Read the following story:

Imagine that there is in this room [or wherever your group most often meets] *a large gray elephant. The elephant stands there, shifting from one foot to another and slowly swaying from side to side. Imagine also in this room the people with whom you regularly meet — your associates in this group. You watch as these people carefully walk around the elephant. They avoid the gigantic swaying body and the swinging trunk and try to carry on their routine activities. Since no one ever talks about the elephant, you know that you're not supposed to talk about it either. And you don't.*

But sometimes you wonder why nobody is doing anything to move the elephant. After all, it's very big, and it's very hard to keep walking around it all the time, and people are getting tired and irritated. You wonder if there is something wrong with you. But you keep wondering, keep walking around it, keep worrying, and keep wishing that there was somebody to talk to about the elephant.

From *Elephant in the Living Room,* by Jill M. Hastings/Marian H. Typpo. Copyright 1994 by Hazelden. Reprinted by permission of Hazelden Foundation, Center City, MN.

- Now explain, "The elephant is a metaphor for the unspoken issues in this group. Can you identify the elephants in this group? In doing so,
  ⇒ describe the issue you are labeling as an elephant;
  ⇒ provide a brief explanation of why you view that particular issue as an elephant; and
  ⇒ suggest how you could possibly remove the elephant from the room."

- Once the group has identified the elephant and established ways of dealing with it, pose the following questions:
  ⇒ Based on your elephant, what issues need to be addressed?
  ⇒ What changes need to be made?

VARIATION:
- This exercise may be used to identify sensitive issues such as prejudice, bullying, or competitive behavior.

FACILITATORS' NOTES / TIPS
- A work group's "elephant" may be an unproductive member, an autocratic leader, or poor working conditions. A dominant or a silent member may hamper the progress of a therapy group. In a family, it might be an alcoholic or drug-dependent parent or child, a critical parent, or a terminally ill member.
- This exercise has been used in family therapy with a substance abuser whom no one dared to confront and with bereaved families where there is a conspiracy of silence around the death.

YOUR NOTES:

WHAT'S YOUR SCREEN? DEVELOPING SENSITIVITY

OBJECTIVE:
- To increase group members' awareness of how they are influenced by the behaviors of others.

MATERIALS:
- Blackboard, flip-chart, overhead projector, or individual handouts containing vignettes about fictional group members. Some samples follow:
  ⇒ In a group, Jennifer suddenly changed the subject without explanation.
  ⇒ Every time Frank made a comment in a group he kept his eyes focused on the leader's face.
  ⇒ As the group discussion progressed, Joe became more and more tense and restless. Finally, Joe abruptly got up and left the room, saying nothing.
  ⇒ In a group, Brenda, who had been talking a lot, suddenly became silent.
  ⇒ John is consistently ten to thirty minutes late for each meeting.
- Pen and paper for each participant to record answers

TIME REQUIRED:
- One hour

GROUP SIZE:
- No more than fifteen

PROCESS:
- Say, "You have before you five vignettes about fictional group members. Each situation points out a nonverbal expression of feelings by a particular person. For each situation, please write down *two* different feelings that might have given rise to such behavior.

- After group members have responded to the vignettes, introduce the term "screen" to them, explaining as follows: "Each of us has a *screen* based on our past experiences, our family values, and the influences of our culture and society. This screen impacts on our perceptions of others. To help you obtain a clearer picture of your particular screen, think about what screens may be influencing your feelings about each of the people in the vignettes."

- Provide ten minutes for members to consider this question. Then direct participants to find two other people and discuss their responses and ideas with them. Remind them to ensure that each person in their group has an opportunity to speak. Forewarn participants that the larger group will reconvene in fifteen minutes.

- When the larger group has reassembled, ask:
  ⇒ Has your view of each of the individuals in *this* group changed? In what way? Why?
  ⇒ What have you learned about yourself and your screens?
  ⇒ What understanding have you gained about how you might be influenced by the behaviors of others in groups?
  ⇒ How will you use this knowledge in the future?

VARIATIONS:
- Create vignettes based on issues or concerns arising within your group or on current media topics.
- Vignettes can be role played. (Time required may need to be altered to accommodate this.)
- If your goal is to examine cultural diversity, racism, or discrimination, adapt the vignettes to include other races or minorities. For example, Jennifer may be a young Hispanic, or Frank might be physically disabled.

FACILITATORS' NOTES / TIPS
- You might place the definition of a screen and the follow-up questions on a flip-chart or overhead. Reveal them one by one.

YOUR NOTES:

CENTER STAGE:
SHARING THE LIMELIGHT

OBJECTIVES:
- To provide each group member with the opportunity to be heard.
- To give group members opportunities to express and clarify, without interruption, their individual viewpoints.
- To enhance members' listening skills and show them how to draw information from a speaker.
- To create an environment whereby listeners are challenged to be objective about viewpoints that are contrary to their own.

MATERIALS:
- No special materials

TIME REQUIRED:
- Five minutes per group member

GROUP SIZE:
- Ten to one hundred, subdivided into smaller groups, each consisting of three to five people

PROCESS:
- As facilitator, choose a topic for discussion that is relevant to your group. A class, for example, might discuss capital punishment, abortion, censorship, ethics, sex, drugs, or feminism. Family issues which provoke discussion range from household chores to children's privileges, from rights and responsibilities of family members to financial concerns. Particular group concerns may be reactions to fees, responsibilities of members, use of time, or special projects.

- Say, "Now that you are in smaller groups, choose a *focus person* who will be the first member to give a reaction to the discussion topic. That person will voice his or her reaction for five minutes, without interruption. The task of the remaining group members is to understand the speaker through the use of minimal verbal and nonverbal encouragers, such as 'Yes,' 'Uh-huh,' 'Tell me more,' and head-nodding. After five minutes, group members may respond by asking questions or making statements, but *only after they have paraphrased* the focus person's viewpoint to that person's satisfaction."

- Rotate the role of the focus person until each member is given the opportunity to assume the role.

- Reconvene the larger group and lead a discussion of the following:
  ⇒ What was it like to be the focus person?
  ⇒ What was it like to be the listener?
  ⇒ What obstacles or blocks to effective listening can you identify?
  ⇒ How can you apply what you have learned to your everyday life?

VARIATIONS:
- Group members may choose the topic to be discussed.
- Besides developing listening and speaking skills, group members might benefit from focusing on content, especially if they are struggling with particular societal, family, or group problems. In that case, once each group member has had the opportunity to be focus person, direct the larger group to collaboratively summarize the ideas presented and suggest courses of action.

FACILITATORS' NOTES / TIPS
- More outspoken, assertive members often overshadow reticent ones in group environments, causing them to feel "lost in the crowd." This exercise provides an opportunity for children and disadvantaged, shy, and minority group members to be heard without interruption.

YOUR NOTES:

THE BELT:
PRACTICING BRAINSTORMING

OBJECTIVES:
- To free up conventional or habitual thinking.
- To help group members look at alternative solutions.
- To provide some fun and give variety to a program.

MATERIALS:
- Blackboard or flip-chart and chalk or marker
- Paper and pencil for each group member

TIME REQUIRED:
- Thirty minutes to one hour, depending on group size

GROUP SIZE:
- Subdivide large groups into smaller ones, each consisting of eight or ten people

PROCESS:
- Say, "People often find themselves stuck using one or two methods of dealing with problems. This exercise will help you to broaden your perspective."

- Set the scenario: "Imagine that you are stranded on a desert island. You *really want* to get off this island because you believe it is dangerous. You are not only frightened, but also lonely. You miss your family and friends. You have no equipment with you except for your *belt*."

- Explain the exercise: "Brainstorm with the others in your group for three to five minutes about how you could use your belt. Remember, in brainstorming, you do not discuss the merits of each suggestion. Appoint one person to record *all* of your group's suggestions, no matter how absurd they might seem. Continue suggesting until the time allotted runs out."

- When the five minutes have passed, say, "Vote for your group's three best solutions. Write them on the flip-chart [or blackboard], so that your solutions can be presented to the larger group."

- After this, solicit group members' responses to the following questions:
  ⇒ What solutions are realistic?

⇒ What particular insights did you derive from this activity?

⇒ In what way was some of your thinking challenged?

⇒ How might you apply brainstorming to other activities within this group? to your work experience? to your everyday family life?

VARIATION:

• After this warm-up exercise, participants will be ready to brainstorm a problem relevant to your group.

FACILITATORS' NOTES / TIPS

• We participated in a variation of this exercise at a workshop where college instructors brainstormed exciting solutions to particular instructional problems.

YOUR NOTES:

FISH BOWL 1: OBSERVING OTHERS

OBJECTIVES:
- To provide an opportunity for members to receive feedback about their behavior in groups.
- To enhance both individual and group observational skills.
- To provide members with the opportunity of giving helpful feedback, particularly when members have become stuck on an issue.

MATERIALS:
- No special materials

TIME REQUIRED:
- Up to one hour

GROUP SIZE:
- Subdivide a large group into groups of four to six people, and then pair them so that two groups of four to six work together.

PROCESS:
- Direct the paired groups to form two circles, one inside the other. Then say, "Each of you in the outer circle, choose one member of the inner circle whom you will directly observe." Ensure that every person in the inner circle has an observer.

- Assign the group in the inner circle the task of planning a party, a presentation, or a project. The task of the outer circle is to observe and provide feedback to those in the inner group based on the following criteria:
  ⇒ Nonverbal behaviors such as eye contact, gestures, facial expressions, body movement, and posture;
  ⇒ Number of times the "partner" whom they are observing spoke; and
  ⇒ Nature of interaction
      a. defining problems
      b. seeking/giving information
      c. seeking/giving opinions
      d. encouraging
      e. leading
      f. following
      g. making peace
      h. disrupting

      i.   digressing
      j.   initiating
      k.   clarifying.

- After five minutes, invite the inner group to pair with its observers and discuss their observations. Encourage observers to give *positive* feedback. If negative feedback is absolutely necessary, it *must* be supported by clear behavioral descriptors. Allow five to ten minutes for this feedback. Then say, "The observer group will now become the inner circle [or the observed]. Repeat the same planning process, after which the new outer group will provide individual feedback."

VARIATION:
- Videotape a group at work and then invite members to engage in a self-evaluation process.

FACILITATORS' NOTES / TIPS
- Choose the topic for discussion carefully to minimize stress. Humorous, light-hearted topics are effective. Or you might focus participants on an on-going concern that the group might like to discuss.

***YOUR* NOTES:**

THE FISH BOWL 2: FINDING A VOICE

OBJECTIVES:
- To encourage group members who feel unheard or powerless to find their own voice.
- To provide an environment where people can be heard without interruption or distraction.

MATERIALS:
- Chairs, arranged in a circle

TIME REQUIRED:
- One hour (fifteen minutes for inner group discussion, plus fifteen more for outer group discussion, and thirty minutes for general discussion)

GROUP SIZE:
- Varies with the nature of the concern

PROCESS:
- Say, "Those group members with particular concerns, find chairs and create a circle in the center of the room. The rest of the group will form a circle around the inner circle. For the next fifteen minutes, the inner group will discuss their concerns while the outer group silently observes. This is done according to the following guidelines:
  ⇒ Speakers should be as clear and specific as possible.
  ⇒ People in the outer circle must remain verbally and nonverbally silent.
  ⇒ All participants should strive to maintain a problem-solving, rather than adversarial, stance.
  The overall goal is to develop understanding and work toward solutions."

- After fifteen minutes, the inner and outer circles switch positions, and the process is repeated with the second group responding to the inner group's concerns.

- During the final thirty minutes, the total group reconvenes to react to the process and seek solutions to the concerns.

VARIATION:
- Timelines may be altered to fit particular situations. Groups may require another fifteen-minute sequence before they are ready to reconvene.

FACILITATORS' NOTES / TIPS
- A useful guide to the problem-solving process is outlined in several group work books (Corey & Corey, 1997; Toseland & Rivas, 1997; Zastrow, 1993).
- This exercise could be useful when working with groups whose members reflect a broad range of concerns. Such groups might contain parents and children, students and teachers, employers and employees, or minorities and majorities.

***YOUR* NOTES:**

SOLUTION CIRCLE:
CONSIDERING FEEDBACK

Adapted from an exercise by Jean Illsley Clarke
International Workshop Leader

OBJECTIVE:

- To provide a structured format for offering feedback to group members faced with perplexing problems (for example, student study groups; parenting groups; or new immigrant groups who are dealing with problems such as stress, time management, dealing with anger, or cultural adjustment).

MATERIALS:

- Paper for each group member
- Pen or pencil for each person

TIME REQUIRED:

- Three to ten minutes per person

GROUP SIZE:

- Subdivide larger groups into groups of six to eight people, seated in circles

PROCESS:

- Say, "Each of you, think of a problem you are experiencing, one that is related to the group purpose. You will, in turn, become your group's focus person, and present your particular concern to the others. Then members will each offer, in one sentence, their solutions to that concern. The member seated to the left of the focus person will record each solution as it is given. The focus person will simply listen to each proposed solution and thank the person who supplied it. The thank you is for the person's willingness to share the idea, not a comment on the quality of the solution. As a group member, you have a right to pass on offering a problem or suggesting a solution, and you may offer your problem or suggestion later -- after some of the others have spoken."

- At the end of the round, invite each focus person to consider the suggestions offered and report to the larger group on his or her plans for their implementation.

- This exercise is complete when each member has taken a turn as focus person.

VARIATION:

- If a concern is sensitive, the focus person may choose to receive the solutions in writing.

FACILITATORS' NOTES / TIPS

- Reticent members or those whose first language is other than that of most group members will feel less intimidated if they are given an opportunity to write their solutions before sharing them.
- When the total group reconvenes for the next meeting, you might ask members to report on the solutions they have *implemented*.

***YOUR* NOTES:**

DREAM CATCHER: SETTING GOALS

Adapted from an exercise by Wilma Rubens, B.Sc., Dip. Ed.
Freelance Group Facilitator

OBJECTIVE:
- To develop individual and group goals.

MATERIALS:
- Blackboard, flip-chart, or overhead projector
- Sheet of paper for each participant
- Pens, crayons, markers

TIME REQUIRED:
- One hour

GROUP SIZE:
- Subdivide larger groups into groups of eight to ten people

PROCESS:
- As you demonstrate on the blackboard or flip-chart, say, "Print your name in the middle of your sheet of paper and divide the paper into four equal quadrants.

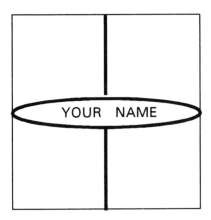

- "In the quadrants, draw a picture or describe in writing the following:
  - ⇒ In the upper left quadrant, your roles in life or characteristics about yourself.
  - ⇒ In the lower left quadrant, a dream, wish, or goal you have for yourself. *Think big!*
  - ⇒ In the upper right quadrant, the barriers that are preventing you from reaching your dream or goal.
  - ⇒ In the lower right quadrant, indicate how this group might help you to reach your goal.

- "When you have completed your dream catcher diagram, find a partner and share your findings. Move on to another partner until you have spoken with every person in your small group. One of your tasks in this sharing is to develop individual and group goals which you will bring back to the larger group. When we reconvene, I will record your ideas on the flip-chart [or blackboard] and, from them, we can develop group goals."

VARIATION:

- By changing the components of your group's dream catchers, you can use this exercise in various ways. In developing what you ask of participants, keep in mind that each quadrant of the dream catcher has a particular purpose.
    - ⇒ The upper left quadrant describes the person, and might be illustrated by having them draw or describe a favorite song, book, movie, pet, or scene.
    - ⇒ The lower left represents the dream or goal which is related to the overall purpose of the group.
    - ⇒ The upper right illustrates the barriers or blocks to achieving the goal.
    - ⇒ The lower right shows the group's role in meeting the goal.

FACILITATORS' NOTES / TIPS

- We have serendipitously discovered this exercise to be a useful gauge of our progress in compiling this book.

YOUR NOTES:

Chapter 4

Middle Phase and Transitions

In the middle phase of group activity, members know one another, expectations have been clarified, and a sense of group identity is emerging. It is an exciting time where productive work occurs. As facilitator, you essentially "call your group to work." Your primary thrust is to motivate and assist group members to achieve both individual and group goals. This can be challenging, however, because

- group sessions become more complex and demanding;
- participants' spirits may flag and their goals may seem to be too distant;
- the increased expectation of member involvement may feel threatening to participants; and
- members may resist the facilitator's directions, forcing you to seem more demanding and less supportive than in earlier phases of group activity.

Tuckman (1965) identifies four stages of group development: *forming*, *storming*, *norming*, and *performing*. The points listed above are part of the storming and norming phases.

You might address participants' concerns about this middle phase by:

- dealing directly with any difficulties that arise;

- administering a mid-phase evaluation (see page 153);

- encouraging risk taking;

- stressing the rewards that accompany active involvement;

- beginning with a short relaxation exercise to focus members and facilitate their participation;

- engaging members in exercises that encourage interpersonal communication;

- meeting individually with problematic members; and

- considering a change in the group venue (for example, a group may be invigorated by planning and participating in a day trip or by having a guest speaker).

If group facilitation becomes difficult, consultation with a trusted colleague may provide you with much-needed support.

BREATHING LESSONS:
RELAXATION EXERCISES

OBJECTIVE:
- Use this exercise and its variations to help members become more relaxed and focused. Although useful at any time during a group's life, this exercise is most effective before or after discussion of sensitive or difficult material.

MATERIALS:
- If you use background music, you will require a tape or CD player and tape or disk.

TIME REQUIRED:
- Five to fifteen minutes

GROUP SIZE:
- Any size

PROCESS:
- Teach this easy breathing exercise by speaking in a gentle and well-modulated voice. The dots which follow the phrases below indicate where you should pause and perhaps repeat them. You may also use words of encouragement, such as "Excellent," or "That's it," throughout. (See page 61.)

- With participants either seated, standing, or lying down say, "Place your hands flat against your waist with your middle fingertips touching." (Demonstrate this.) . . . "Begin breathing using your diaphragm and noting how your fingers separate slightly. . . . Now move your breathing up into the lower lobes of your lungs and allow them to fill completely. . . . Finally, move your breathing up into the upper lobes of your lungs, taking in as much breath as possible. . . . If this is done well, you might feel a soreness in your throat.

- "Now reverse the process, slowly eliminating all the air from your upper lung lobes, your lower lobes, and your diaphragm. . . . When you think you have eliminated all the air, breathe out some more until *all* the old air is completely gone. . . . Your fingertips should come together when you have exhaled completely."

- Watch the group closely as you speak, so that you can adjust your speech to their breathing rhythm.

VARIATIONS:
- Use the easy breathing exercise above as a precursor to these variations:
  ⇒ Say, "Make yourself comfortable, ensuring that your legs and arms are not crossed. . . . Remove your glasses and loosen clothing that is constricting. . . . Begin to pay attention to your breathing, and as you do, close your eyes. . . . Now take very deep breaths using the breathing method you've already practiced."
  ⇒ "Take four very deep breaths and notice the physical feelings in your arms and hands. . . . You may notice that your hands tingle a bit as the oxygen reaches every cell in your body, allowing you to relax completely. . . . Begin to breathe normally now, but note how much more relaxed your body feels."
  ⇒ "Take six deep breaths, breathing in through your nose and out through your mouth. . . . Take time to notice your abdomen expand as you fill your lungs with air. . . . Breathe in relaxation and breathe out tension."
  ⇒ Encourage participants to visualize in detail a pleasant scene – a tropical isle, a mountain meadow, a beach, or a restful room in a house. Suggest that they use *all* of their senses – seeing, hearing , smelling, touching, tasting. For example, "Come with me to a beautiful tropical island. Hear the waves lapping against the shore, the cries of the gulls. Smell the salt air. You can almost taste it. Feel the warm sun on your skin." Help group members to capture in their imaginations the pleasure of actually being there.
  ⇒ "Stand up. . . . Raise your hands above your head. . . . Stretch left and hold 1-2-3-4. . . . Stretch right and hold." Repeat several times.
  ⇒ Hug someone. Three hugs per day are very calming.
  ⇒ Have a good laugh. Share a joke with the group or invite someone to tell one. Make sure that jokes are appropriate.

SIMPLE SOOTHERS:
RELAXATION QUICKIES

Adapted from "Surviving Module"
Department of Social Work, Mount Royal College
Calgary, Canada

OBJECTIVE:

- These short exercises, which can be used at any time during a group meeting, are designed to help members relieve tension and stress.

MATERIALS:

- No special materials

TIME REQUIRED:

- No more than five minutes per exercise

GROUP SIZE:

- Any size

PROCESS:

- Say, "Release the tension from your mouth and eyes and say to yourself, 'Alert mind, calm body.' . . . As you do this, take a deep breath from your abdomen, . . . and when you exhale, let your jaw, tongue, and shoulders go limp. . . . Feel the sense of warmth and heaviness through your body . . . and down into your toes."

VARIATIONS:

- Say, "This short exercise will release your tension from head to toe. Press your tongue hard against the roof of your month as you slowly draw in a deep breath, counting to ten while you do so. . . . Feel the tension build. . . . Now allow your tongue, your jaws, and your shoulders to go limp as you exhale. . . . Feel the tension leave your body."
- Say, "When experiencing stress, our hands and feet may feel cold. When this happens, bring your hands together and rub them briskly. Then let them float down towards your thighs. You are taking with them the sensation of warmth. As you do this, you will notice that this warm feeling is telegraphed all the way down to your feet."
- Say, "When experiencing 'performance anxiety,' take a moment to wet your lips – this diverts your mind from worrying. Then say to yourself, 'Calm and relaxed,' as you take a deep breath from your abdomen."

RELAXATION SCRIPT: PASSIVE PROGRESSIVE RELAXATION

OBJECTIVE:
- Use passive progressive relaxation to help group members feel calm and settled.

MATERIALS:
- No special materials other than space to lie down, if possible

TIME REQUIRED:
- Up to fifteen minutes

GROUP SIZE:
- Any size

PROCESS:
- Say, "Start by taking five nice big breaths. . . . Start with your diaphragm. . . . *Feel* the air as it expands your diaphragm. . . . Now move up to the lower lobes of your lungs. . . . Good. . . . Great. . . . Now take the air to the upper lobes of your lungs. . . . *Fill* your lungs completely. . . . Excellent. . . . Now let the air out. . . first from the upper lobes . . . now from the lower lobes. . . now the diaphragm. . . . Good. . . . Do that four more times, and while you do, *breathe in relaxation* . . . and *breathe out tension*. . . . Feel your hands as you do. . . . You might feel a tingling in your hands as the oxygen reaches every cell in your body . . . . Good. . . . Just keep breathing deeply. . . . Deeper and deeper. . . . Relaxed.

- "Now that you're beginning to relax, I'd like you to pay attention to the top of your head. . . . Feel the muscles relax. . . . Now move down into your forehead. . . . Allow all the muscles in your forehead to relax. . . . Feel your eyes becoming heavier and heavier . . . so very, very heavy . . . that you almost feel you couldn't open them if you tried . . . very heavy. . . . Good. Gently relax, moving down your face and the sides of your head. . . . Relax those muscles completely. . . . Feel your jaw. . . . Allow your jaw muscles to give up their hold. . . . Don't try to force anything. . . . Just allow them to relax and give up their hold. . . . You may find you have to swallow or scratch an itchy spot. Just allow yourself to do that. . . . Everything you do will help you to become more and more deeply relaxed. . . . You may hear noises around you . . . people talking, doors closing, the ceiling fan motor. . . . Don't try to push those sounds away. . . . Just relax and stay connected to my voice. . . . Every noise you hear will help you to become more . . . and more deeply relaxed.

- "Pay attention to your neck and shoulders. . . . Allow all the muscles there to relax completely. Imagine your shoulders sagging down into the mat [rug, pillow] . . . as your relaxation goes deeper and deeper. . . . Now take your relaxation down into your upper arms. . . . Let it flow gently down through your elbows, into your forearms, and right into your wrists. . . . Good. . . . Now, just imagine for a moment that your arms and hands are becoming heavier and heavier. . . . You may notice they're also becoming warmer . . . so very warm . . . as you become more and more deeply relaxed.

- "Return to your shoulders now, and begin to let your relaxation flow gently down through your upper back and chest. . . . Feel all the muscles giving up their hold completely as you become more and more relaxed. . . . Take your relaxation down and down through your torso, past your waist. . . . Let those muscles relax completely. . . . Continue down, and down through your buttocks and groin, and into your thighs. . . . Feel your thigh muscles relaxing. . . . Let the warm feeling flow gently down through your knees. . . into your calves and shins . . . past your ankles . . . and into your feet. . . . Allow your legs to become heavier and heavier. . . . Feel them becoming warmer and warmer . . . so very heavy and so very warm. . . deeper and deeper relaxed.

- "Now your body is beautifully and completely relaxed. . . . Feel your body. . . . Memorize these feelings of deep and complete relaxation. . . . It feels so good.

- "When you're ready, bring yourself back to this time and space. . . . Allow your arms and legs to lose their heaviness, so that when you open your eyes, you'll feel perfectly normal, but wonderfully relaxed."

FACILITATORS' NOTES / TIPS:

- This may be used either at the beginning or end of a group session, but it's particularly effective just before participants go home.
- Ideally, participants should be lying down for this exercise, but where settings are not conducive to this, it may be done in a sitting position. However, people's necks should be supported, because heads tend to sag as relaxation progresses.
- Your voice should be low, soft, and well-modulated. Don't rush. Allow plenty of time between phrases. Key words in phrases should be elongated and gently repeated.
- Some participants relax so much that they fall asleep, and some of these may snore loudly. If this happens, just carry on as though nothing unusual is happening.   Only the people in the snorer's immediate vicinity are affected, and some of these won't even notice the sound.
- Any reference you make to noises should reflect the noises heard in the room (For example, say, "You may hear people in the hall, doors opening and closing, the ceiling fan motor, or even sounds from outdoors. . . . Don't be concerned. . . . Just let these sounds float in and out of your consciousness. . . . Everything you hear will help you become more and more deeply relaxed.").
- This script can be a precursor to deeper levels of relaxation through visualization.

YOUR NOTES:

WAKE UP! SHAKE UP! AN ENERGIZER

OBJECTIVE:
- After lunch or an intensive work period, participants may need to be energized. Use this exercise to invigorate your group and to promote laughter.

MATERIALS:
- No special materials

TIME REQUIRED:
- Three or four minutes

GROUP SIZE:
- Any size

PROCESS:
- Say, "Please stand and form a circle facing inward toward the center. Now turn to your right and begin to pat the back of the person in front of you. Use a loose-wristed slapping rather than a punching. Allow your pats to become more intense and rhythmical. You want to stimulate the blood flow, so make your pats hard enough to do that, without hurting the person, of course. Notice the feeling of stimulation in the muscles in your own back as you are patted."

VARIATIONS:
- Instead of asking participants to pat their neighbors' backs, have them use massage.
- Use background music to help participants maintain rhythm and enjoy the experience.
- Invite group members to stand, and, using their left elbows, write their individual names in the air. Then have them repeat the exercise using their right feet. They might also continue writing, using their left hips, noses, etc. as writing tools.

FACILITATORS' NOTES / TIPS:
- WARNING: Preface this exercise by stating that those who have back problems or a sensitivity to being touched may sit out this exercise if they wish to do so.

YOUR NOTES:

MYSTERIOUS HAPPENINGS:
AN ENERGIZER

OBJECTIVE:
- This nonthreatening exercise is intended to engage all participants by sharing the solving of a mystery. It promotes laughter, discussion, and compromise, as well as acceptance of and respect for diverse opinions and solutions.

MATERIALS:
- Paper and pen for each subdivided group

TIME REQUIRED:
- Fifteen minutes

GROUP SIZE:
- Subdivide a large group into smaller units of four or five members *after* introducing members to the mystery (see below).

PROCESS:
- Read the story's ending to the group: *"Gilbert and Priscilla are found dead on the floor. Around them are a small puddle of water and bits of broken glass."*

- Now divide the group into subgroups and instruct them, within the next ten to fifteen minutes, to write the beginning of this story. They must tell
    ⇒ who the characters are,
    ⇒ what happened to them, and
    ⇒ how they died.
  Also request that each group select someone from among themselves to read the story that they have created.

- When the groups' stories have been read, reveal your version: *"Gilbert and Priscilla are two goldfish. Their fish bowl shattered after a strong gust of wind blew it off the table."*

FACILITATORS' NOTES / TIPS:
- We were told Judy Guffey (Honolulu, Hawaii) used this exercise with a Polynesian group that loved to tell stories. Their versions of the tale provided group members with an excellent opportunity to practice their English skills.

TRUTH AND LIES:
GETTING TO KNOW ONE ANOTHER

OBJECTIVE:
- This exercise allows group members to become more familiar with one another. Although it is somewhat demanding, it sets up a spirit of conviviality within the group.

MATERIALS:
- No special materials

TIME REQUIRED:
- Fifteen to thirty-five minutes

GROUP SIZE:
- Between four and twenty members who are, ideally, seated in a circle. If there is ample time, this may be done in the large group. However, if time is limited, subdivide it into groups of two or three.

PROCESS:
- Say, "Think of two things that are true about yourself and two things that are lies. One at a time, share these truths and lies. Other group members will then call out their guesses as to which are the truths and which are the lies. Your truths and lies should not be evident." (For example, people who are six feet tall would not claim their height was five feet, one inch.)

FACILITATORS' NOTES / TIPS:
- This exercise is most effective when members have at least some knowledge of one another, as this better equips them to evaluate the truths and the lies.
- When we used this exercise with a group of students, an Asian woman said, "I speak Chinese and I love rollerblading." The "lie" was that she spoke Chinese, but the others in the group guessed it as "true."

YOUR NOTES:

TEMPERATURE CHECK: GATHERING GROUP FEEDBACK

OBJECTIVES:
- Use this exercise to help group members "catch up" with each other and "get things out of the way," therefore enabling them to become focused on the activities of the day.
- Use it as a concluding exercise for the session, an opportunity to receive feedback.

MATERIALS:
- No special materials are needed for the primary exercise. However, some of its variations may require each participant to have a pen and paper.

TIME REQUIRED:
- Decide on a suitable time limit, make the group aware of that limit, and adhere to it. Setting a time limit for this exercise is crucial because otherwise your agenda may become overridden by individual concerns.

GROUP SIZE:
- Any size

PROCESS:
- Say, "On a continuum, with *cold* being 'one' and *hot* being 'ten,' tell us how you are feeling about this group." Repeat this process around the room until all members have spoken.

VARIATIONS:
- Ask group members to rate the following question on a scale of 1 to 10, with 1 being poor and 10 being excellent: "How are you feeling about the group?" Now ask, "What needs to happen in the group for you to move your rating up one point on the scale?"
- Invite members to give a short report on their progress toward their individual goals.
- At the beginning of the meeting, request that members participate in a brief check-in exercise. Say, "If you were to compare our group to a movie or television program, what movie or program would that be, and why?" (At times you might request participants to compare the group with a song, a book, or an animal. Use your creativity to develop a repertoire of these check-in exercises.)

- Use this as a "check-out" exercise. Say, "In a word or two, tell us what this meeting was like for you."
- Invite group members to write out a question or concern on paper and deposit it in a box or basket that you have provided. Tell them, "I will then draw several papers from it and we as a group will collaborate to address the issues. Only a few questions or concerns can be discussed in the time we have available."

FACILITATORS' NOTES / TIPS:

- Request that others in the group not speak while individual members are sharing their views. However, they *may* comment in a *positive* manner after a speaker has finished voicing his or her views.
- We have used this exercise in classroom settings, business meetings, and therapy groups.

YOUR NOTES:

POSITIVE GOSSIPING: PROVIDING INDIVIDUAL FEEDBACK

OBJECTIVE:
- Use this exercise to provide positive feedback to each participant in your group.

MATERIALS:
- No special materials

TIME REQUIRED:
- Two minutes per person

GROUP SIZE:
- Any number of people, subdivided into groups of three or four. (Use this exercise's variation in groups with fewer than ten participants.)

PROCESS:
- Say, "In your small groups, each of you will take a turn at being the focus person while the other two talk about you as though you were not present. When you discuss the other person, you must speak only in *positive* terms. I will indicate the end of each two-minute interval, when it's time to rotate the focus person."

VARIATION:
- Do this exercise within the group without subdividing it. Each group member takes a turn being focus person while all the others discuss him or her.

FACILITATORS' NOTES / TIPS:
- This exercise can be very empowering for group members. It also promotes participants' enthusiasm for the tasks ahead.
- This can also be an effective ending exercise or a means to discuss the departure of one member.

YOUR NOTES:

RECALLING THE PAST:
EVOKING MEMORIES

OBJECTIVES:
- Use this exercise to learn about group members through sharing important past experiences.
- Use it to link people from diverse settings.
- Use it to enhance self-understanding.

MATERIALS:
- Food common to all cultures represented in your group – for example, fruit (especially strawberries), bread, tea, coffee

TIME REQUIRED:
- Two to three minutes per person

GROUP SIZE:
- Ten to twelve

PROCESS:
- Say, "Examine the food and recall a memory it evokes." Then direct members to take turns sharing those memories.

VARIATIONS:
- Use a picture common to all cultures – one of a schoolhouse, a pet, a landscape – to evoke discussion.
- Depending on your group's purpose, use a picture that evokes painful memories – a picture of a hospital, for example, in a bereavement group.
- Use a symbol from a cultural tradition related to birth, weddings, and death to evoke scenes from the past.

FACILITATORS' NOTES / TIPS:
- This exercise's versatility is unlimited. And, depending on your group's objectives and the pictures or objects used, it can be a very powerful one, as well. Even the simplest objects can evoke strong positive or negative memories.

YOUR NOTES:

Chapter 5

Teaching Concepts
and
Developing Skills

What I hear, I forget
What I see, I remember.
What I do, I understand.
Confucious, 400 B.C.

Learning is more effective when it is an active rather than passive process because people retain more of what they learn when using their senses – hearing, seeing, smelling, tasting, and touching.   Further engagement through talking and doing enhances learning even more.   The illustrations on the next page depict retention rates for active and passive learning.

Adapted from *Educating for a Change* by R. Arnold, B. Burke, C. James, D. Martin, and B. Thoma copyright Between the Lines and the Doris Marshall Institute, 1991. Used by permission.

The exercises in this chapter provide:

*   methods of introducing new information to participants;

*   opportunities for participants to increase self-awareness and other awareness; and

*   an environment for expanding a repertoire of new behaviors.

When using these exercises, we suggest that you:

*   clearly explain how the exercise relates to the information being presented;

*   be aware that you need to deal with the emotional impact of the exercises; and

*   allow time within the sessions for reflection and discussion.

THE FEELINGS CHARADE: ROLE PLAYING EMOTIONS AND SITUATIONS

OBJECTIVE:
- Approximately 90% of our communication is said to be nonverbal. Although one might argue with percentages, the significance of such communication cannot be underestimated. This exercise is designed to develop participants' awareness of nonverbal communication.

MATERIALS:
- Container (e.g., a basket)
- Slips of paper, on each of which you have printed a word representing an emotion (e.g., anger, boredom, frustration, joy)

TIME REQUIRED:
- One or two minutes for each scenario

GROUP SIZE:
- Any number up to twenty members

PROCESS:
- Say, "Our first volunteer will begin by selecting one slip of paper from the basket and then acting out the emotion identified on it. When you think you know what emotion is being enacted, call your answer out to the group."

- Explain that after group members have identified a particular emotion, they will discuss how they have experienced the emotion themselves and observed it expressed by others.

- Give each group member the opportunity to enact the emotion he or she chooses from the basket.

VARIATIONS:
- To summarize this exercise, ask participants:
  ⇒ What effect did acting out the emotion have on you?
  ⇒ How did another's portrayal of a particular emotion affect you?
  ⇒ What did you learn from this exercise?

⇒ How can you apply this learning in your work and/or your everyday life?

- Provide each group member with a statement (e.g., "I was fired from my job." "I just found out I was pregnant." "I'm bored with retirement." "You made me mad."). Each person then role plays the emotions associated with the particular experience he or she has selected.

- Invite couples or families to sculpt problematic situations that evoke intense emotions. Then direct them to resculpt the scene to reflect a more positive outcome. (See Facilitators' Notes)

- When working with members from diverse groups (e.g. people of varying cultures, ages, sexual orientations, abilities, and disabilities) invite each person to sculpt the particular emotion he or she selects. Follow this with a discussion on the similarities and differences of expression among people.

- Use this exercise to role play potentially stressful situations, so that participants may learn, for example, to nonverbally express self-confidence at a job interview or during an oral presentation. Invite group members to point out the effects of hand gestures, eye movements, stance, and other non-verbal indicators.

FACILITATORS' NOTES / TIPS:

- The difference between *acting out* and *sculpting* is that acting out requires movement, whereas sculpting involves the sculptor creating a scene to his or her satisfaction and then freezing it.

YOUR NOTES:

PICK A WORD, ANY WORD: LEARNING TERMS AND JARGON

OBJECTIVE:
- Often people in new situations do not understand some of the words they are hearing. This exercise is designed to enhance understanding of the jargon associated with the group. This can be used in a broad range of groups where new information is being introduced, such as
  ⇒ support groups based on illness, bereavement, family violence, or child abuse;
  ⇒ immigrant groups wanting to learn the idioms of the new culture; and
  ⇒ classroom groups, particularly where technical information is being taught.

MATERIALS:
- Container (e.g., a basket)
- Slips of paper on which you have written unfamiliar and commonly used words or phrases that are specific to the content of your group sessions
- Pens or pencils
- Paper
- Resource materials such as dictionaries, textbooks, and/or manuals

TIME REQUIRED:
- Time required depends on the number of words or terms you choose to use.

GROUP SIZE:
- Fifteen to twenty members

PROCESS:
- Place the slips of paper in the container and explain, "In this basket are words or phrases that are important for you to know in order to achieve maximum benefit from this group. Break up into sub-groups of two or three and choose a slip of paper from the basket. Then, referring to your resource book, define the term written on your paper. Discuss your definition with your teammates to arrive at a common understanding of the term. Now create a meaningful sentence using the term."

• Invite subgroups to present their definitions and sentences to the larger group, where their findings will be further discussed.

VARIATION:

• Assign each group member a word or term to research as homework and then present to the group for discussion at the next session.

FACILITATORS' NOTES / TIPS:

• Allow ample time for discussion to ensure that all members develop a clear understanding of the terminology.
• You may reserve time to clarify pertinent vocabulary at the beginning of a meeting or devote an entire session to this activity.
• Suggest that members maintain an ongoing card file or notebook of relevant definitions.
• This exercise may require more time for new immigrant groups unfamiliar with the many English-language idioms.

***YOUR* NOTES:**

COMPLETE THE SENTENCE:
INTRODUCING A TOPIC OR COURSE

OBJECTIVES:
- To introduce group members to concepts relevant to a topic or course.
- To help group members, not only to become acquainted with each other, but also to share ideas.

MATERIALS:
- Container (e.g., a basket)
- Slips of paper on which you have reproduced sentences from a relevant text or handout, cut in half and placed in the container. (Include half as many sentences as there are people in your group.)

TIME REQUIRED:
- Twenty to thirty minutes

GROUP SIZE:
- Any even number up to thirty

PROCESS:
- Say, "In this container are pieces of paper, each containing half a sentence from _____ . [Name the source text or handout.] Each of you, choose a slip of paper and find the person who holds the other paper which completes your sentence. Together with your partner, read, discuss, and then briefly present the ideas from information collected to the rest of the group."

VARIATION:
- Use half pictures or diagrams in the same way.

FACILITATORS' NOTES / TIPS:
- This exercise requires some forethought and preparation; therefore, it is not appropriate for use by a "last-minute" facilitator.
- It is, however, particularly useful for reviewing course or group objectives.

YOUR NOTES:

THE LAUNCHING:
ENGAGING PARTICIPANTS
IN A DISCUSSION

OBJECTIVE:

- Group members often require a transition period before beginning discussion of a new topic. This exercise invites them to review their knowledge on the subject and to consider their ongoing learning needs.

MATERIALS:

- Paper
- Pens or pencils

TIME REQUIRED:

- Ten to thirty minutes

GROUP SIZE:

- Any size

PROCESS:

- Request participants to respond on paper to the following questions about the new topic to be introduced:
  - ⇒ What do I know about this subject?
  - ⇒ What worries me about a discussion of this subject?
  - ⇒ What am I looking forward to learning about the topic?
  - ⇒ What do I still need to learn about it?

- Invite them to share their responses with the group.

VARIATION:

- Collect the responses and, with group members' permission, use them for ongoing group planning.

FACILITATORS' NOTES / TIPS:

- A large group may require subdivision.
- The information gathered in these responses can provide you with valuable insights into the particular needs of group members.
- Develop your own questions to suit your group's objectives.

YOUR NOTES:

FREEWRITING: EXPLORING A SUBJECT

OBJECTIVE:
- Freewriting is a way of introducing a new topic or facilitating further exploration of thoughts and feelings about a subject.

MATERIALS:
- Paper
- Pens or pencils

TIME REQUIRED:
- Five to fifteen minutes

GROUP SIZE:
- Any size

PROCESS:
- Distribute writing materials and explain, "Today we will explore _____.   [Name the subject – sexuality, cross-cultural issues, violence, your job, your work environment.] For the next ten minutes, write whatever comes into your mind about the subject. Don't stop to ponder or think. Just keep writing as much as you can get down. If you get stuck, keep writing – write 'I'm stuck,' or 'I don't know what else to write.' Keep your pen moving. I'll warn you when eight minutes have elapsed."

- Inform group members that their writing will be confidential: "What you write will neither be read by anyone else, nor be discussed."

VARIATION:
- Forego the discussion of confidentiality and direct group members to discuss their notes within small groups or the entire group (if the latter is not too large).

FACILITATORS' NOTES / TIPS:
- Freewriting can be used at any time in the group process.
- Be aware that freewriting may be inhibited by the participants' knowledge that the content of their notes will be discussed.
- By enhancing their confidence in the journal writing process (see pages 16 and 17), this exercise may benefit those who are hesitant to set their thoughts down in journals.

THE PARTICIPANT AS TEACHER: SHARING THE LOAD

OBJECTIVE:
- Presenting information to a group requires a thorough understanding of the subject matter. This exercise provides a teaching opportunity which will heighten individual and group learning.

MATERIALS:
- Stimulating reading material that is relevant to your group's purpose
- Flip-chart, blackboard, or overhead projector
- Colored markers or chalk

TIME REQUIRED:
- Twenty minutes for small group discussion and planning of the presentation, plus ten minutes presentation time for each group

GROUP SIZE:
- Twenty to twenty-five members, subdivided into groups of four or five

PROCESS:
- At the meeting prior to presentation, subdivide the group, providing each small group member with reading material. Request that they read the information for homework, keeping in mind that they will discuss and organize it with their subgroup and present it to the larger group at the next meeting.

- At the second meeting, say, "Join your small group to discuss and summarize the main points of your assigned reading. Write these points on the blackboard [flip-chart, overhead]. Then each group will present its material to the larger group. Be prepared to answer whatever questions may arise."

FACILITATORS' NOTES / TIPS:
- While the groups are preparing their summaries, be available to clarify concepts and offer presentation suggestions.
- Help participants recognize the importance of using audiovisual aids, such as a flip-chart. Displaying presenters' work helps them to articulate their ideas more clearly.

CHINESE PRACTICE: PRACTICING ASSERTIVENESS IN PUBLIC SPEAKING

Adapted from an exercise by Luree Hays
Kamehameha Schools and Kapi'olani Community College
Honolulu, Hawaii

OBJECTIVES:
- To encourage assertiveness in public speaking.
- To energize the group.

MATERIALS:
- Three-by-five-inch note cards
- Pens or pencils
- Moveable chairs

TIME REQUIRED:
- Ten to fifteen minutes

GROUP SIZE:
- Twenty to thirty participants

PROCESS:
- At the meeting prior to this activity, announce, "At our next meeting we will do an exercise that will help you present information. Before that time, choose a topic that is relevant to the group, develop an outline of your presentation, and prepare note cards with key words. Use one card for every two minutes of speaking."

- For the presentations meeting, arrange the chairs in a large circle. When the group has convened, say to them, "Take out your note cards (*not* your outlines) and stand behind your chairs facing the center of the room. When I say, 'Go!' begin your speeches, *all at the same time*. I will walk around the circle calling out encouragement to you as you speak. . . Ready. . . Set . . . Go!"

- Your feedback as facilitator may consist of words and phrases such as,
    - ⇒ "Concentrate."
    - ⇒ "Be vigorous."
    - ⇒ "Speak louder."
    - ⇒ "Smile."
    - ⇒ "Look at your audience."

⇒ "Be sincere."

⇒ "Stand tall."

Be sure to accompany your feedback with positive reinforcers such as, "Great!", "Excellent!", and "Good work!"

VARIATIONS: • Luree Hayes reported that this exercise is particularly useful for teaching a new language. Students learning Chinese, for example, walk around the classroom or with a friend, reciting their lessons aloud. Periodically, their teacher walks with one, then another, listening and correcting errors.

FACILITATORS' NOTES / TIPS: • This is a *very* noisy exercise, but members usually leave the session feeling good about themselves and optimistic about their speeches. The commotion eases the self-consciousness aroused by a listening audience.

YOUR NOTES:

MIND READING:
JUMPING TO CONCLUSIONS

OBJECTIVES:
- To help participants understand the pitfalls of jumping to conclusions.
- To encourage participants to stop, listen, and resist mind-reading or making assumptions.

MATERIALS:
- No special materials

TIME REQUIRED:
- Ten minutes in the dyad (five for each member), plus twenty minutes for discussion

GROUP SIZE:
- Any size, subdivided into groups of two

PROCESS:
- Say, "One of you will begin to talk about an incident that occurred recently, but will stop telling the story at an appropriate juncture. For example, you might say, 'I went over to visit my mother to discuss her birthday plans. My mother . . .' or 'I went on an extensive tour with my friend. We . . .". Then it will be your partner's turn to speak, completing the scenario as he or she believes it will end. Do not interrupt one another."

- Indicate when the five minutes allotted to the first person has elapsed, so that the second one has a chance to speak.

- After the second person finishes speaking, direct the original storyteller to reveal what actually happened. Then ask the partners to compare notes and answer the following questions:
  ⇒ How similar were your stories?
  ⇒ How is this exercise reflective of what happens in everyday communication?
  ⇒ What have you learned from this exercise?
  ⇒ How can you apply your new knowledge in your life?
  ⇒ What was it like to have your mind read?

- Repeat this exercise, reversing the roles of the two storytellers.

- Conclude the activity by reconvening the larger group for a general discussion of the questions above.

**FACILITATORS'
NOTES / TIPS:**

- This exercise is particularly useful for teaching listening skills.

***YOUR* NOTES:**

DIRTY WORDS:
LOOKING AT UNCOMFORTABLE WORDS

OBJECTIVE:
- This lighthearted exercise is designed to introduce an awkward or embarrassing subject.

MATERIALS:
- Flip-chart (blackboard, or overhead projector)
- Marker or chalk

TIME REQUIRED:
- Thirty minutes

GROUP SIZE:
- Up to twenty members

PROCESS:
- Say, "To be able to effectively deal with some words that will be spoken during these group sessions, we need to become accustomed to hearing and saying them without embarrassment. Each time I speak a word from my list, you're asked to call out synonyms for it or the positive and negative connotations that come to mind. For example, the word 'sex' may bring forth words like 'fun,' 'creative,' or 'dirty.' I will write my word on the flip-chart [blackboard or overhead] and record your answers. Once our brainstormed list is complete, we can have a general discussion about the patterns we see."

VARIATION:
- As lists are created, categories may emerge. Write these on a flip-chart, blackboard, or overhead. Each participant then indicates which category his or her particular word falls into. Record each answer in the appropriate category. For example, the word "sex" may evoke words which can be grouped under the headings "male," "female," and "both."

FACILITATORS' NOTES / TIPS:
- This exercise depends on you, the facilitator, having a high level of comfort with the embarrassing words.
- If group members speak the words, they eventually become desensitized toward them.
- This exercise is effective with diverse groups who are seeking to understand common stereotypes associated with particular cultural groups, disabilities, or sexual orientations.

SIMULATION FOR STIMULATION: ROLE PLAYING A CONFLICT

OBJECTIVE:
- To provide opportunities for group members to role play a conflict situation and practice constructive outcomes.

MATERIALS:
- Scenarios provided by you or by participants
- Areas for small groups to gather

TIME REQUIRED:
- Ten minutes to one hour

GROUP SIZE:
- Any size, subdivided according to the number of actors and observers required for the scenarios

PROCESS:
- Say, "Based on the particular scenario you will be role playing, form groups. Ensure that each group has enough members for all the roles of a particular scenario, as well as at least one observer. Role play the conflict described to you, discuss possible solutions, and role play the solutions. After thirty minutes, everyone will reassemble in the larger group to discuss questions, concerns, and new insights about your experiences."

VARIATIONS:
- Suggest a scenario and solicit volunteers to role play it in front of the entire group.
- Recording the role plays and replaying the video for the group adds depth to the experience because the actors are able to see and/or hear how they use their voices, facial expressions, and body gestures. Be advised that this activity will increase the amount of time required to complete the exercise.

FACILITATORS' NOTES / TIPS:
- Although this exercise focuses on role playing a conflict, it can also be used in other situations, such as preparing for job interviews, facilitating adaptation to a new culture, or practicing effective parenting skills.

YOUR NOTES:

Chapter 6

Values

Value, according to the dictionary, is something desirable, worthy, or right – such as a belief, standard, or moral precept. This chapter presents exercises which offer opportunities for participants to identify and reflect on their values. The activities will also assist them to:

- explore the impact of personal values on behaviors and feelings;
- develop a clearer understanding of their own values and beliefs;
- check their beliefs against their actions;
- understand how their personal values may be an obstacle to their being accepted and respected;
- examine conflicting values and make decisions about those that no longer fit their beliefs; and
- realize how diverse backgrounds influence values.

To effectively use these exercises, you, as facilitator, should:

- be aware of your own values and how they impact the group;
- be vigilant to some participants' tendency to use avoidance strategies, whereby they focus on the values and beliefs of others

and try to change them, rather than reflecting on their own values;

- create an environment of support and acceptance because group members may experience intense emotional reactions; and

- provide time for participants to reflect on the meaning of the exercise.

PRIVACY ZONE:
DISCOVERING PATTERNS
OF SELF-DISCLOSURE

OBJECTIVE:
- To encourage participants to examine their patterns of self-disclosure, consider their personal boundaries, and develop new boundaries where applicable.

MATERIALS:
- Individual copies of the Privacy Chart and Questions (see pages 91 and 92)
- Pens and pencils

TIME REQUIRED:
- One hour

GROUP SIZE:
- Any size, divided into triads for discussion

PROCESS:
- After distributing a copy of the Privacy Chart and Questions to each group member, say, "The various circles on the chart represent degrees of intimacy, with the innermost circle being your self. The next circle represents people with whom you share intimate information (such as your best pal, your lover, or your family) and the outer circle, those with whom you are least intimate (such as an acquaintance or a stranger). On the question sheet you will find a series of questions followed by a *key word*. To answer the questions, write the key word in your circle of choice. For example, when considering whom you would tell about your favorite television program, print *TV* in the circle of your choice. Now take some time to examine your emerging patterns of self-disclosure and self-containment."

- When participants have completed their charts, direct them to form into groups of three and discuss the following questions, which may be displayed on a flip-chart, overhead, or blackboard:
  ⇒ What did you learn about your patterns of self-disclosure?
  ⇒ What did you discover about your personal boundaries?

⇒ What changes do you wish to make to these boundaries?

VARIATION:

- Use this exercise to examine personal relationships. In this case, leave the *key word* column blank on the questionnaire. Thus, rather than directing group members to write down the key words, request that they write down the *names of people* whom they might tell about particular topics. They may then transfer these names to the appropriate circles on their privacy chart.

FACILITATORS' NOTES / TIPS:

- Discussion is an essential element in this exercise because it exposes participants to differing patterns of self-disclosure and self-containment, thereby promoting increasing acceptance of others' values and beliefs.

YOUR NOTES:

PRIVACY CHART

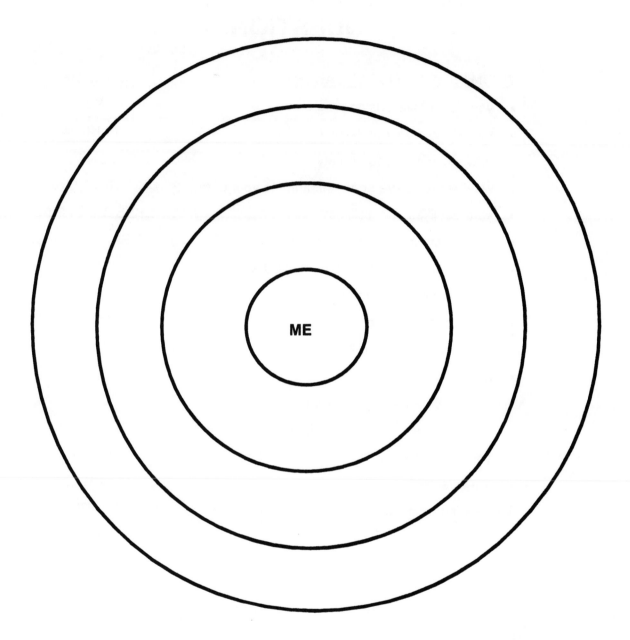

See next page for questions.

PRIVACY ZONE:
DISCOVERING PATTERNS OF SELF-DISCLOSURE
QUESTIONS

WHOM WOULD YOU TELL ABOUT:	KEY WORD
• your favorite television program?	TV
• your doubts about religion?	RELIGION
• how you spend your money?	MONEY
• whether you have been unfaithful to your partner?	UNFAITHFULNESS
• your pet likes and dislikes?	LIKES & DISLIKES
• your most embarrassing moment?	EMBARRASSING
• the last time you had a speeding ticket?	TICKET
• a major problem in the marriage?	MARRIAGE
• your salary?	SALARY
• your health problems?	HEALTH
• an abortion?	ABORTION
• the last time you cried and why?	CRY
• your favorite and least favorite teacher and why?	TEACHER
• your favorite food?	FOOD
• the weather?	WEATHER
• your innermost desires?	DESIRES
• your address?	ADDRESS

MIRACLE WORKERS:
CLARIFYING ONE'S VALUES

OBJECTIVE:
- To invite members to reflect on important values by asking them to choose from various attractive alternatives.

MATERIALS:
- Worksheet containing the names of fifteen miracle workers (see pages 95 and 96)
- Pens or pencils
- Flip-chart, overhead, or blackboard containing the discussion questions

TIME REQUIRED:
- Thirty to forty minutes

GROUP SIZE:
- Any size, with subdivisions of three or four for discussion

PROCESS:
- Distribute the worksheets, one to each participant, and say, "Working alone, choose the five miracle workers you value the most – that is, the five whose gifts you would most like to receive. Once you have done that, pick five more miracle workers whose work you value. You are then left with the five people who form your least desirable group."

- Ask participants to consider the following questions: For each grouping,
    ⇒ Why did you make the selections you did?
    ⇒ What seems to link together the five most desirable people you chose? the five least desirable?
    ⇒ What values are you upholding in your choices?
    ⇒ Are there any choices that seem out of place with the others in a particular grouping?

- Now invite them to break up into groups of three or four and discuss the questions.

- After this discussion, request that participants draw up a list of the things they are doing or could do in their lives that are similar to what their top five miracle workers are doing.

- Finally, say, "Consider that each of you is a miracle worker. Make a self-contract based on this exercise. What miracles do you want to strive for? Where can you begin? How can we help one another reach our goals?"

VARIATION:

- Group members can role play the miracle workers, with each person arguing for why he or she is more powerful, more needed, or more useful than the others.

FACILITATORS' NOTES / TIPS:

- The noise and joking evoked by this exercise may be distracting to some; therefore, your challenge is to help participants focus on the primary purpose of this exercise, which is to get in touch with important values.

***YOUR* NOTES:**

MIRACLE WORKERS: CLARIFYING ONE'S VALUES
WORKSHEET

A group of fifteen experts, considered miracle workers by those who used their services, have agreed to provide these services for the members of this group. Their extraordinary skills are guaranteed to be 100% effective. It is up to you to decide which of these people can best provide you with what you want.

Dr. Dorian Gray   A noted plastic surgeon, he can make you look exactly as you want to look by means of a new painless technique. (He also uses hormones to alter body structures and size!) Your ideal physical appearance can be a reality.

Baron Von Barrons   A college placement and job placement expert. The college or job of your choice, in the location of your choice, will be yours!

Jedediah Methuselah   He guarantees you long life (to the age of 200) with your aging process slowed down proportionately. For example, at the age of 60 you will look and feel like 20.

Drs. Masters Johnson and Fanny Hill   Experts in the area of sexual relations, they guarantee that you will be the perfect male or female, will enjoy sex, and will bring pleasure to others.

Dr. Yin Yang   An "organismic" expert, she will provide you with perfect health and protection from physical injury throughout your life.

Dr. Knot Not Ginott   An expert in dealing with parents, he guarantees that you will never have any problems with your parents again. They will accept your values and your behavior. You will be free from control and badgering.

Stu Denpower   An expert on authority, he will make sure that you are never again bothered by authorities. His services will make you immune from all control which you consider unfair by the school, the police, and the government (including the armed forces).

"Pop" Larity	He guarantees that you will have the friends you want now and in the future. You will find it easy to approach those you like and they will also find you easily approachable.
Dr. Samantha Smart	She will develop your common sense and your intelligence to a level in excess of 150 IQ. It will remain at this level through your entire lifetime.
Rocky Fellah	Wealth will be yours, with guaranteed schemes for earning millions within weeks.
Dwight D. DeGawl	This world-famed leadership expert will train you quickly. You will be listened to, looked up to, and respected by those around you.
Dr. Otto Curnegy	You will be well-liked by all and will never be lonely. A life filled with love will be yours.
Dr. Claire Voyant	All of your questions about the future will be answered, continually, through the training of this soothsayer.
Dr. Hinnah Self	She guarantees that you will have self-knowledge, self-liking, self-respect, and self-confidence. True self-assurance will be yours.
Prof. Val U. Clear	With her help, you will always know what you want, and you will be completely clear on all the muddy issues of these confused days.

THREE CHARACTERS:
CLARIFYING ONE'S VALUES

OBJECTIVE:
- To clarify and enhance participants' awareness of their own goals and purposes in life by identifying with the achievements and characteristics of others.

MATERIALS:
- Paper
- Pens or pencils

TIME REQUIRED:
- Thirty to forty minutes

GROUP SIZE:
- Any size, with subdivisions of three to five people

PROCESS:
- Say, "Think of people in real life, the news, or history, or characters in literature, fiction, and cartoons – people who, if you could be someone other than yourself, you would like to be. Write down the names of the three people or characters whom you would *most* like to be and explain why you would like to be these individuals."

- Then request group members to write down the names of the three people or characters whom they would *least* like to be, and explain why.

- Now ask them to form small groups of three to five members and share their lists and explanations. Remind them, "In this exercise people are revealing a lot about themselves through their character choices. To ridicule someone's character choice is to ridicule the person, so please be tactful in your responses to others."

VARIATION:
- Do the same exercise using animals instead of people as characters.

FACILITATORS' NOTES / TIPS:
- Participants will feel more comfortable sharing their characters if a certain degree of trust exists; therefore, allow participants to choose and form their own groups. Also allow individuals to pass – to refrain from discussion – whenever they wish.

CATASTROPHE STRIKES! MAKING THE LEAST WORST DECISION

OBJECTIVE:
- To help group members
  - ⇒ clarify personal values,
  - ⇒ develop problem-solving skills, and
  - ⇒ listen to the ideas of others with a view toward compromise.

MATERIALS:
- Individual copies of the "Least Worst Decision Worksheet" (see page 100)
- Pens or pencils

TIME REQUIRED:
- One to two hours

GROUP SIZE:
- Up to fifteen participants in a single group
- With larger groups, subdivide participants into groups of fewer than fifteen for problem solving and discussion.

PROCESS:
- Distribute the worksheets and direct participants to read the story "Catastrophe Strikes!" including the list of survivors.

- Say, "Referring to your list, first decide for yourself who should survive. Be prepared to justify your choices and your eliminations to the larger group. Try to develop a consensus for your decision within the larger group."

- After the group's discussion as to who should survive, ask participants to consider and discuss the following with one another:
  - ⇒ Identify the different values that you became aware of through participation in this exercise.
  - ⇒ What did you learn about your own and others' problem-solving skills?
  - ⇒ What creative compromises captured your imagination?

VARIATIONS:

- Conduct the exercise using the following story:

  Five people are boating. In the boat, there are a father – a fifty-five-year-old heart specialist reputed to be the best in the country; his thirty-six-year-old wife – a dermatologist; their eight-year-old child; their neighbor – a forty-three-year-old industrial salesman for a major corporation; and his wife – a thirty-five-year-old former model who appears frequently in local television commercials. If some tragedy occurred and only one of the five could be saved, who should it be?

- Use your imagination to make up a story that is suitable for your particular group.

FACILITATORS' NOTES / TIPS:

- You may find that some group members may protest participation in exercises involving life and death decisions. Acknowledging their concerns and discussing them within the group will generally reduce anxiety and encourage active participation.
- Some interesting discussions may result from assumptions that are made about the age, gender, or other characteristics of survivors.

***YOUR* NOTES:**

VALUES: THE LEAST WORST DECISION WORKSHEET

CATASTROPHE STRIKES!

An environmental catastrophe has occurred. Except for a two-hundred-acre parcel of land and twelve people, all vegetation and human life has been destroyed. At the moment, this parcel of land can sustain only eight human lives. However, there is a possibility that land can be reclaimed.

The twelve initial survivors are:

- *a 17-year-old boy who is a high school dropout and whose girlfriend is pregnant*
- *his 15-year-old girlfriend who suffers from epileptic seizures*
- *a 49-year-old black preacher*
- *a 29-year-old non-English-speaking Asian plant biologist with expertise in plant genetics*
- *a 38-year-old doctor who is unable to have children*
- *a teacher who is homosexual*
- *a 36-year-old former prostitute who has been "retired" for four years*
- *a 48-year-old male artist who is an ex-convict; he served three years for dealing drugs (including prescription drugs) and is still on parole*
- *a 40-year-old ex-RCMP officer who cannot be separated from his gun*
- *a politician who lives in the most prestigious part of town*
- *a 26-year-old male business administrator*
- *the business administrator's 25-year-old wife who has spent the past nine months in a mental institution and is still under heavy sedation; they refuse to be separated*

WHAT'S *MOST* IMPORTANT?: EXPLORING ONE'S VALUE SYSTEM

OBJECTIVES:
- To clarify one's own values.
- To develop an awareness of the values of others.

MATERIALS:
- Individual copies of "Values Survey A" (see page 103)
- Pens or pencils
- Scissors for "Values Survey D" variation

TIME REQUIRED:
- One hour

GROUP SIZE:
- Any size; subdivided for discussion

PROCESS:
- Distribute the "Values Survey A" to each participant and say, "Go through the values listed on the handout and choose the ten that are the most important to you. The list is merely a starting point. Feel free to add other values to it. . . . Now rank the values you have chosen, with *1* being your most important value."

- Ask participants to create subgroups of three or four persons and share the results of the exercise with one another. Allow ten minutes for discussion.

- Then ask group members to consider the questions below and share their reflections with their subgroup. You might display the questions on a flipchart, overhead, or blackboard, or reproduce individual copies from the bottom of page 106.
  - ⇒ How did your values influence your choice of employment?
  - ⇒ How do your values influence your work performance?
  - ⇒ How do your values affect, in a negative and a positive way, your personal relationships?
  - ⇒ What did you learn from this exercise?
  - ⇒ What surprised you about it?
  - ⇒ What might you do differently as a result of this exercise?

VARIATIONS:

- See pages 104 and 105 for two "Values Survey" variations, "B" and "C."
- Detach the "Values Survey D" from the discussion questions (see page 106) and distribute copies of the survey, along with scissors, to all group members. Direct them to cut out their fifteen "value slips." Next, have them sort through the values and "throw out" the five that they deem relatively unimportant, retaining the ten values that are personally most meaningful to them. When this task is completed, ask participants for their general reactions. Then instruct them to discard five *more* value slips. When all have done this, have them break into subgroups to discuss the exercise. Now distribute the questions (lower section of page 106) and direct group members to reflect on and discuss them.

FACILITATORS' NOTES / TIPS:

- You might modify the values and/or the questions to more directly address the needs of a specific group or community.

***YOUR* NOTES:**

WHAT'S *MOST* IMPORTANT?
EXPLORING ONE'S VALUE SYSTEM

VALUES SURVEY A

_____	LEARNING	_____	SECURITY
_____	OPENNESS	_____	ROUTINE
_____	INDEPENDENCE	_____	FAMILY
_____	ACCOMPLISHMENT	_____	MONEY
_____	ORGANIZATION	_____	GOOD TIMES
_____	INTIMACY	_____	ME
_____	CLEANLINESS	_____	SPIRITUALITY
_____	CONFLICT	_____	SEX
_____	COOPERATION	_____	FRIENDS
_____	STATUS	_____	GOOD HEALTH
_____	_____	_____	_____
_____	_____	_____	_____
_____	_____	_____	_____
_____	_____	_____	_____
_____	_____	_____	_____

(Write your own values.)

WHAT'S *MOST* IMPORTANT?
EXPLORING ONE'S VALUE SYSTEM

VALUES SURVEY B

_____ LOYALTY: maintaining important connections and commitments

_____ POWER: having authority and influence

_____ INDEPENDENCE: having freedom of thought and action

_____ EDUCATION: continuing growth in knowledge and skills

_____ RECOGNITION: receiving recognition for achievements

_____ EMOTIONAL WELL-BEING: solving emotional problems and maintaining self-esteem

_____ SPIRITUAL WELL-BEING: living according to my spiritual beliefs

_____ PHYSICAL WELL-BEING: taking care of my body

_____ SEXUAL FULFILLMENT: feeling good about myself sexually

_____ QUALITY MARRIAGE OR RELATIONSHIP: having a marriage or relationship that is a source of love and fulfillment

_____ LOVE: loving and being loved

_____ SUCCESS AND ACHIEVEMENT: being able to do things really well

_____ PLEASURE OR JOY: enjoying the joys and pleasures in my life

_____ FAMILY: maintaining family traditions and background

_____ PARENTHOOD: having and taking care of children as a source of fulfillment

_____ AESTHETICS: having beauty in my surroundings

_____ ACCEPTANCE: being accepted by people who are important to me

_____ _____

_____ _____

(Write your own values.)

WHAT'S *MOST* IMPORTANT?
EXPLORING ONE'S VALUE SYSTEM
VALUES SURVEY C

_____ To rid the world of prejudice

_____ To serve the sick and needy

_____ To become a famous figure (movie star, sports hero, etc.)

_____ To have a year of daily massages and the finest food from the world's best chef

_____ To know the meaning of life

_____ To set your own working conditions

_____ To be the richest person in the world

_____ To have the perfect love affair

_____ To be leader of the most powerful country on earth

_____ To be the most attractive person in the world

_____ To have a house overlooking the most beautiful view of the world, in which you may keep for one year forty of your favorite works of art

_____ To live to be a hundred years old, with no illness

_____ To master the profession of your choice

_____ To have a vaccine that makes all persons incapable of lying or graft

_____ To control the destinies of 500,000 people

_____ To have the love and admiration of the whole world

_____ To have an anti-hang-up pill

_____ To have your own all-knowing computer, which will give you any and all facts you might need

_____ To spend six months with the greatest religious figure of your faith, past or present

_____ To _____

_____ To _____

(Write your own values.)

WHAT'S *MOST* IMPORTANT?
EXPLORING ONE'S VALUE SYSTEM

VALUES SURVEY D

Cut along the dotted lines:

COMMITMENT	FAMILY	FRIENDSHIP
FULFILLMENT	HEALTH	HELPING OTHERS
HONESTY	INDEPENDENCE	LOVE
LOYALTY	RELIGION	RESPECT
SECURITY	STATUS	TRUST

QUESTIONS FOR DISCUSSION

- How did your values influence your choice of employment?

- How do your values influence your work performance?

- How do your values affect, in a negative and a positive way, your personal relationships?

- What did you learn from this exercise?

- What surprised you about it?

- What might you do differently as a result of this exercise?

THE IDEAL PIE DEAL:
DEVELOPING SELF-AWARENESS

OBJECTIVES:
- To pictorially represent daily activities.
- To consider desired changes in one's life.
- To develop alternative strategies for goal attainment.

MATERIALS:
- Paper
- Pencils (preferably pencil crayons); pens are not recommended because of the creative nature of this exercise
- Erasers

TIME REQUIRED:
- Twenty to thirty minutes

GROUP SIZE:
- Any size

PROCESS:
- Invite group members to each take a colored pencil and draw a large circle or pie on his or her sheet of paper. Say, "Your circle represents a twenty-four-hour day. Now divide it into hours spent in typical activities. You may wish to list your activities and the amount of time you spend at them before beginning to 'slice your pie' into segments. For example, your pie may consist of education, work, sleep, friends, chores, family, cultural activities, time alone, and/or recreation. Be sure to label each slice."

- When participants have completed their diagrams, have them consider the following questions:
  ⇒ How satisfied are you with the divisions of your pie? On a scale of 1 to 10, with 1 being dissatisfied and 10 being completely satisfied, rate your satisfaction with the hours allotted to the activities you have specified.
  ⇒ Ideally, what size would you want each slice to be?

- Now direct participants to draw their ideal pies – what they would *like* their typical day to contain.

- Ask participants:
  - ⇒ What can you do to move toward your ideal pie?

VARIATIONS:
- Subdivide the group and invite members to discuss their drawings with one another.
- Direct participants to draw several pies – perhaps one for each day of their week, or one for their weekend and another for their weekdays.
- Rather than drawing a pie that depicts their activities, participants might do so according to the time they spend in various roles. For example, one might be a mother, a colleague, a sibling, a child, a wage earner, and so on. Segments are based on a certain percentage of the time they have available.

FACILITATORS' NOTES / TIPS:
- With or without discussion, this exercise is very effective in achieving its objectives.

YOUR NOTES:

WHERE DO I STAND?
DECLARING ONE'S VALUES

OBJECTIVE:
- To encourage participants to consider and declare their personal values.

MATERIALS:
- Three poster board signs taped at different areas in the room: one reads YES, the second NO, and the third EITHER WAY

TIME REQUIRED:
- Forty-five to sixty minutes, including discussion time

GROUP SIZE:
- Up to twenty participants

PROCESS:
- Say, "In response to each statement that I read, move to the sign which represents your answer. For example, if you agree with the statement, stand by the YES sign; if you disagree, go to NO; and if you are uncertain, stand by EITHER WAY."

- Read the first statement below. When all who are participating in the exercise have moved to their chosen locations, invite some of them to briefly tell the group why they made their particular choices.

- Read each of the other statements, one at a time, questioning participants' responses in the same way. The statements are as follows:
  - ⇒ Children should be spanked.
  - ⇒ Blowing over 0.08 on a breathalyzer test should be a criminal offense.
  - ⇒ The father in a home should have the final word.
  - ⇒ People who steal are criminals.
  - ⇒ Children should be sent to church.
  - ⇒ Parents are largely responsible for their children's behavior.
  - ⇒ Gun control is an essential part of a safe society.
  - ⇒ A man who stays at home with his children is afraid of the real world.
  - ⇒ Cats should be leashed.

⇒ Gambling (bingo halls, casinos) should not be the primary source of funding for charitable organizations.

VARIATIONS:
- Develop statements which are relevant to your group's subject area.
- After completing the activity above, pose the following questions to the whole group:
  ⇒ How did you come to hold your belief?
  ⇒ How do you act upon your values?
  ⇒ What is your view of others holding differing values?
  ⇒ Were you surprised to see who stood with you? To see who stood on the opposite side?

FACILITATORS' NOTES / TIPS:
- Because people move around the room, this exercise is energizing as well as fun.

YOUR NOTES:

Chapter 7

Self-Enhancement

The exercises in this chapter are designed to facilitate the group participants' understanding of themselves and others, thereby encouraging individual growth. Personal growth occurs when group members:

- witness the progress of other group members;
- learn to trust and value others;
- learn to accept challenge; and
- learn to provide and accept feedback, empathy, and support.

Specifically, these exercises will help group members

- explore and re-evaluate life issues;
- examine emotions and attitudes which lead to changes in behavior;
- consider relationship issues; and
- enhance self-assessment and self-valuing skills.

When forced to choose between the competing needs for safety and personal growth, people usually opt for safety. Because group members are asked to share private aspects of themselves in the following activities, the facilitator must be sensitive to their need to feel safe. Some group members will not risk their vulnerability to fully engage in the exercises unless you can create an atmosphere of trust within the group. You can do this by modeling attentive, inclusive behavior and by encouraging group members to give and receive feedback respectfully and without judgment.

DEFINING YOUR SPACE: EXPLORING PERSONAL BOUNDARIES

Adapted from Integrative Body Psychotherapy
Carol Hechtenthal, M.S.W., IBP Instructor
Calgary, Canada

OBJECTIVE:
- To provide stimuli for expanding group members' personal boundaries or personal space.

MATERIALS:
- Large room with ample space for participants to move about freely
- Tape recorder and musical tape (Bette Midler's *Wind Beneath My Wings* is a good one.)

TIME REQUIRED:
- Five minutes

GROUP SIZE:
- Any size, space permitting

PROCESS:
- Say, "Find a spot in which you can move your body freely without interfering with anyone else's movements, and stand in it. Without moving your feet, allow your body to sway to the music. Extend your arms and begin to define your personal space by moving your arms in every direction. Reach as far as you can, allowing your sense of power to emerge."

- Interject encouragement to participants throughout this exercise – "Reach." "Expand." "Stretch out as far as you can." "Flow." "Fly."

- After a few moments or when the music ends, solicit participants' responses to the following questions:
  ⇒ What was it like for you to expand your personal boundaries?
  ⇒ What have you learned from this exercise that you can apply to everyday experiences?

VARIATION:
- In diverse groups, members' personal boundaries may differ from one another. For example, being wheelchair-bound may limit one's space, and people from differing cultures may define their personal space in various ways. Discussing these differences

as they become evident can lead group members to new insights.

FACILITATORS' NOTES / TIPS:

- When you ask individuals to reach beyond their comfort zone, they may feel threatened; therefore, ensure that your encouragement is enthusiastic, but not demanding.

YOUR NOTES:

BOUNDARIES:
FINDING YOUR COMFORT ZONE

OBJECTIVE:
- Depending on the nature of our relationship, we define how physically close people can come to us. This exercise helps individuals explore and define their personal boundaries and space in relation to others.

MATERIALS:
- No special materials

TIME REQUIRED:
- Five minutes per participant

GROUP SIZE:
- Any size

PROCESS:
- Say, "Find a partner and stand approximately ten feet apart from him or her. One of you remain stationary while the other slowly moves toward you, all the while maintaining eye contact with you. When the stationary partner begins to feel uncomfortable, tell the other, 'Stop.' The distance which is established when you say, 'Stop,' is your personal boundary in relation to your partner."

- Direct partners to reverse their roles and repeat the exercise, and then to choose new partners. Participants should perform the activity with at least four other people.

- Now invite participants to reflect on and discuss the following questions:
    - ⇒ What did you learn from this exercise?
    - ⇒ Did you notice any pattern to the closeness or distance you established with different people? For example, did your personal boundary or comfort vary with the gender of your partner? With the size?

VARIATIONS:
- You will need some chalk and chairs for the participants in this variation. Subdivide the group into dyads, with one partner sitting on a chair, mentally establishing a boundary around himself or

herself, then drawing it on the floor with chalk. The other person then begins to walk toward the circle until told to stop. The participant in the chair now compares the distance to his or her partner with the circle drawn on the floor. What does this reveal?

- Instruct the moving partner to continue on into the personal space of the other person. Have them reverse roles and repeat the exercise. Then discuss the following questions:
  ⇒ What was it like to be the interloper?
  ⇒ How did you feel about having your personal boundary violated?
  ⇒ How did you react? How did you handle it?
  ⇒ What did you learn from this exercise?

FACILITATORS'
NOTES / TIPS:

- For participants who are familiar with each other, this exercise can reveal relationship dynamics which were not previously evident. For example, issues of trust and cultural diversity may emerge and need to be discussed.

YOUR **NOTES:**

THE COLLAGE: SEEING WHO YOU ARE

OBJECTIVES:
- To develop a visual representation of specific aspects of a participant's life.
- To enhance self-awareness and the awareness of the impact of life events.

MATERIALS:
- Large sheets of construction paper
- Picture-filled magazines, wall-paper samples, fabric scraps, craft supplies
- Scissors
- Glue
- Colored markers, pencils, crayons

TIME REQUIRED:
- One hour for creating the collage, plus ten to fifteen minutes per participant for telling his or her story

GROUP SIZE:
- Up to ten participants

PROCESS:
- Randomly lay out the materials on a large table or the floor. Then invite each group member to choose a sheet of construction paper and a pair of scissors. Say, "Construct a collage that represents you and your life, using the materials before you. You might cut out pictures, colors, facial expressions, and words from the magazines, and shapes from the cloth and wallpaper. Use your imagination and have fun! We will later reassemble and give you the opportunity to share your masterpiece with the group."

- When all have completed their collages, reassemble the group for presentations.

VARIATIONS:
- After distributing the construction paper, direct group members to fold their sheets in half, top to bottom, and then in half again, side to side. Their folded papers will resemble greeting cards. Now invite each person to construct a collage, using *both* sides of the construction paper. The outside of the "card" (front and back) will represent the exterior or the self that others see. The inside pages (which usually contain a greeting) will represent a person's private

or secret self, and the back of these four areas (the folded part that most people don't open) will represent what one believes about himself or herself.

- At a previous meeting, ask participants to bring a plain, empty shoe (or similar sized) box or a plain paper bag to this session. Direct them to create collages in which the outside of the box or bag illustrates how they represent themselves to others and the inside depicts their private or hidden selves. They may attach the materials to the outside of the container, but simply place those representing their private selves inside it.

- Direct group members to temporarily affix pictures to their collages with small pieces of tape. After they have shared their creations and told their stories, provide time for them to rearrange their pictures, and/or add new ones which reflect a more ideal representation of their lives, and then glue them down.

- Use the collage project to assist group members in creating narratives about specific experiences, such as the death of a loved one, adjustment to a new culture, life as a member of a minority group, adaptation to marriage, living with a disabling condition, and so on.

FACILITATORS' NOTES / TIPS:

- Sharing their collages may be threatening to some participants; therefore, assure them that they need only share what they feel comfortable discussing.

- Decorating stores may donate old wallpaper sample books to you.

YOUR NOTES:

WHERE DO I FEEL?
CONNECTING MIND AND BODY

OBJECTIVE:
- To help individuals discover where in their bodies they experience particular feelings.

MATERIALS:
- Individual copies of "The Mind-Body Connection Worksheet" (see page 120)
- Crayons

TIME REQUIRED:
- Ten minutes

GROUP SIZE:
- Any size

PROCESS:
- Distribute the worksheet and introduce the exercise by saying, "We have all heard of 'the Mind-Body Connection' and have experienced physical sensations when we have intense feelings. On your handout is a list of feeling words. Using crayons, fill in the word squares with the colors that represent those emotions. As you do so, think about where in your body you experience each of the feelings listed. For example, where do you feel anger? -- in your neck? your hands? your jaw?"

- When that task is completed, say, "The figure on your worksheet represents you. Match your color coding in the feelings squares to that figure. In other words, color the location on the worksheet figure where you feel a particular emotion with the color you have chosen for that emotion. When you have completed the exercise, reflect on what you learned about yourself."

VARIATIONS:
- Ask participants to write in a journal the insights that have emerged from this activity.
- Subdivide participants into groups of two or three for discussing their findings.

FACILITATORS' NOTES / TIPS:
- Because there is vulnerability in exposing one's feelings, an atmosphere of trust *must* exist if people discuss their insights (as in the second variation).

"THE MIND-BODY CONNECTION" WORKSHEET

ANXIOUS ☐

HAPPY ☐

ANGRY ☐

SAD ☐

LOVE ☐

GUILTY ☐

JEALOUS ☐

FRIGHTENED ☐

OFF-THE-WALL SOLUTIONS: SOLVING PROBLEMS CREATIVELY

OBJECTIVE:
- To provide opportunities for people to look at problems and solutions from a fresh perspective.

MATERIALS:
- Paper cut into small strips: three strips per participant
- Three containers, labeled PROBLEM, SOLUTION, and IDEAL OUTCOME, to hold the paper strips

TIME REQUIRED:
- Thirty minutes

GROUP SIZE:
- No more than twenty

PROCESS:
- Say, "On the first piece of paper, write about a problem or stress which is currently affecting your life."   Collect the papers in the container labeled PROBLEM.

- Say, "On the second piece of paper, write one way you have tried to solve your problem." Collect these papers in the container labeled SOLUTION.

- Say, "On your third piece of paper, write the ideal outcome of your problem." Collect these responses in the container labeled IDEAL OUTCOME.

- Now shuffle the contents of the containers and direct participants to take a paper from each of them. As they do so, ask them to read the three-part scenario aloud to the entire group. The problems and solutions will probably be unrelated, but they may blend in a surprisingly relevant and amusing fashion.

FACILITATORS' NOTES / TIPS:
- This fun-filled interlude can provide the impetus for creative problem solving.

YOUR NOTES:

HAPPY AFFIRMATION TO YOU! CELEBRATING SPECIAL OCCASIONS

OBJECTIVE:
- To celebrate special occasions such as birthdays or graduations through positive affirmation.

MATERIALS:
- Paper
- Pencils or pens

TIME REQUIRED:
- One to three minutes per group member

GROUP SIZE:
- Any size, depending on time available

PROCESS:
- Invite each group member:
    ⇒ to share a positive memory about the person being celebrated; *or*
    ⇒ to provide a positive affirmation, spoken aloud to the honored person; *or*
    ⇒ to write a wish to the honored person and present it to him or her.

VARIATION:
- Ask each group member to write down two questions for the honored person to answer. Collect the papers, place them in a basket, and then invite the honored person to draw them, one at a time. The guest may choose whether or not to answer the questions drawn. Examples of questions are:
    ⇒ What is your favorite animal and why?
    ⇒ What attributes make you a good friend?
    ⇒ What qualities do you look for in a friend?
    ⇒ What would you like to be doing in five years?
    ⇒ Who influenced your life?

FACILITATORS' NOTES / TIPS:
- Although honored guests may experience some initial discomfort, they usually enjoy the attention that such a celebration conveys.

YOUR NOTES:

WHERE DO I GO FROM HERE? ASSESSING ONE'S CURRENT STATUS

OBJECTIVE:
- To provide an opportunity for group members to reassess their current roles or status in a professional or personal situation (i.e., as a patient, an employee, a student, a spouse, etc.).

MATERIALS:
- A list of questions such as the following, written on worksheets or assembled on a flip-chart, overhead, or blackboard:
    ⇒ How do you feel about being a _____ (patient, nurse, chemist, stepmother)?
    ⇒ How did you enter into this role (profession, situation)?
    ⇒ What do you like best about your role (profession, situation)?
    ⇒ If you could change one thing about your role (profession, situation), what would it be?
    ⇒ What can *you* do to bring about the desired change?
- Paper (if questions are not on individual worksheets)
- Pencils or pens

TIME REQUIRED:
- Thirty minutes to one hour, depending on group size

GROUP SIZE:
- Twenty to thirty members, subdivided into dyads

PROCESS:
- Ask participants to respond individually in writing to the questions, then discuss their responses with a partner.

- When the dyads have completed their discussions, reconvene the larger group to share their responses to the last two questions on effecting changes.

VARIATION:
- By slightly altering the questions, you might use this exercise as a mid-point evaluation of progress in classes, on committees, and in organizations. Instruct individual members or subgroups to record their responses on large flip-chart sheets, highlighting important points.   Display these sheets at various

points around the room so that group members have the opportunity to read and consider one another's ideas.

FACILITATORS' NOTES / TIPS:

- Large group discussion of the final two questions is effective because:
    ⇒ public declaration increases commitment to change; and
    ⇒ all group members learn from the solutions presented by others.

YOUR NOTES:

HOW DO I LOVE?
EXAMINING EXPRESSIONS OF LOVE

OBJECTIVE:
- To invite members to explore their ideas about love.

MATERIALS:
- Individual handouts (see page 126) containing the following questions and space for responses:
  ⇒ How do I show love to others?
  ⇒ How do I show love to myself?
  ⇒ How do I stop others from showing love to me?
  ⇒ How do I stop myself from showing love to others?
  ⇒ How do I stop myself from showing love to myself?
  ⇒ What have I learned about myself from my answers above?
  ⇒ What do I need to do now?
- Pencils or pens

TIME REQUIRED:
- Twenty-five to thirty minutes

GROUP SIZE:
- Any size

PROCESS:
- Distribute the handouts and ask group members to write their responses to the questions.

- Then invite them to divide into pairs or small groups of three or four in order to discuss their findings.

VARIATION:
- Substitute other emotions for love. For example, groups focusing on understanding anger, managing anxiety, or working through bereavement might consider questions respectively relating to anger, fear, and grief.

FACILITATORS' NOTES / TIPS:
- Large group discussion topics based on this exercise are limitless. For example, you can explore cultural and gender differences, the influences of one's family and society on emotional expression, or the commonalties and differences amongst members.

HOW DO I LOVE?
EXAMINING EXPRESSIONS OF LOVE
WORKSHEET

- How do I show love to others?

- How do I show love to myself?

- How do I stop others from showing love to me?

- How do I stop myself from showing love to others?

- How do I stop myself from showing love to myself?

- What have I learned about myself from my answers above?

- What do I need to do now?

WEEDING YOUR GARDEN: TAKING STOCK OF HOW ONE LIVES

OBJECTIVES:
- To identify positive personal characteristics.
- To determine strategies of self-care.
- To recognize impediments to self-enhancement.

MATERIALS:
- Blank sheets of paper
- Crayons

TIME REQUIRED:
- Thirty minutes

GROUP SIZE:
- Any size

PROCESS:
- Distribute the paper and crayons, and say, "In the center of your page, draw a small circle and print your name in it. Now draw five petals around the circle, and on each petal write a characteristic you like about yourself. Now draw a stem on the flower and roots. On each root, write something that you do for self-care (for example, your favorite forms of recreation or relaxation). Finally, draw four weeds growing next to the flower. On each weed, write a problem that worries you (these are worries over which you have some control, but about which you have done nothing)."

- When participants have completed their gardens, ask them to reflect on whether they will weed them, and how they might accomplish this.

- Now invite the group to subdivide into groups of three and discuss their pictures.

VARIATIONS:

- Roots might also reflect personal support systems, such as family and friends, and community support systems, such as school and church.
- Minority groups or people with disabilities might label weeds to represent barriers to their full participation in society.
- Drawing a flower of a "significant other" person (i.e., one's parent, spouse, or child) enhances empathy.

SELF-VALUING:
NOTING THE POSITIVES IN ONE'S LIFE

OBJECTIVE:
- To provide an opportunity to look positively at oneself.

MATERIALS:
- Three-by-five-inch or four-by-six-inch index cards (or sheets of paper)
- Pencils or pens

TIME REQUIRED:
- Fifteen to thirty minutes

GROUP SIZE:
- Any size

PROCESS:
- Distribute index cards to all participants. Say, "Draw a small box in the center of your card and print your name in it. From the center of each *side* of your box, draw four lines dividing your card into four quadrants.
  - ⇒ In the *top left* quadrant, write three things you value about yourself.
  - ⇒ In the *top right* quadrant, write three experiences that had value for you.
  - ⇒ In the *bottom left* quadrant, write the names of three people outside your family who value you.
  - ⇒ In the *bottom right* quadrant, write the names of three people within your family who value you."

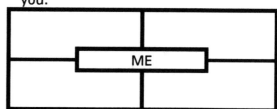

- When participants have completed their cards, direct them to find someone in the group with whom they would like to share the information, and discuss their card with him or her. Encourage members to take enough time to say why each of the situations or people listed is important to them.

SPIDER WEB: IDENTIFYING ACTIVITIES AND RELATIONSHIPS IN ONE'S LIFE

OBJECTIVES:
- To provide a visual representation of significant aspects (activities, relationships) in one's life.
- To provide an opportunity to evaluate one's priorities and limitations.
- To stimulate creative problem solving based on new insights which may lead to productive decision making.

MATERIALS:
- Paper
- Pencils or pens
- Erasers

TIME REQUIRED:
- Thirty to sixty minutes

GROUP SIZE:
- Any size

PROCESS:
- Say, "This activity allows you to see yourself in your drawing of a personal spider web. The web's main radials or arms going out from the center should represent your *attachments* and *involvements* with significant people, places, values, and projects in your life. The transverse threads or those going across the web from one main radial to the other will represent the *activities* that create the unique expressions of your life." You might show the group a *skeletal* diagram such as the one below, but do not inhibit creativity by offering precise directions or examples (such as on page 131).

- Before participants begin to draw, suggest the following: "Take a few moments to think about how you will develop your particular web of life. Then use your creativity, so that your web will be a unique expression of your life. To assist in recall, be sure to name your radials and transverse threads as you proceed."

- When group members have completed their webs, pose the following questions:
    - ⇒ How many of you placed yourselves in the web? What does this tell you?
    - ⇒ How many placed _____ (the purpose or activity of this group) in their web?
    - ⇒ What happens to your web if a main radial disappears (for example, a spouse dies, or one is laid off)? How will you accommodate the loss?
    - ⇒ What if one radial overshadows the other radial threads (you might show this by drawing a very thick radial)? How does this skew one's web?
    - ⇒ What have you learned from constructing your web?

FACILITATORS' NOTES / TIPS:

- Examples of a person's attachments and involvements might include a spouse, parents, children, work, home, and religion. Examples of activities are special occasions, hobbies, club activities, vacations, and social activities. These examples may or may not fit into one's personal web in the ways suggested. Some participants might regard work as a main radial, while others might label it as a transverse thread. Furthermore, the examples are meant to provide *you* with clarification of what might be expected from participants. We do *not* recommend that you share them with group members, as this may interfere with their creativity.

- Note that a mature group may require more time for analysis and discussion, as they are likely to examine their webs in depth.

- In a diverse group, it is interesting to discuss differences related to gender, ethnicity, age, and disability.

SPIDER WEB:
IDENTIFYING ACTIVITIES AND RELATIONSHIPS

EXAMPLES

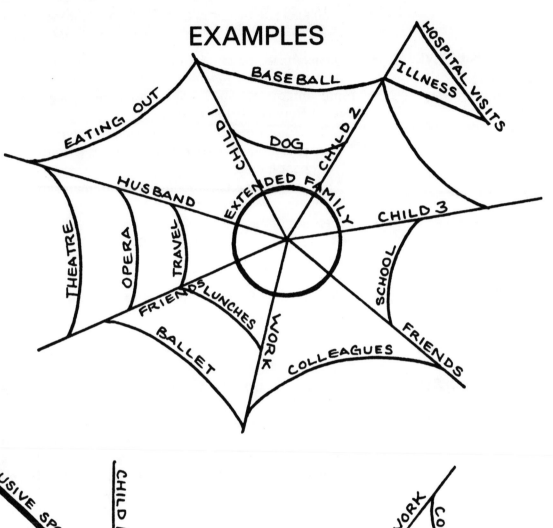

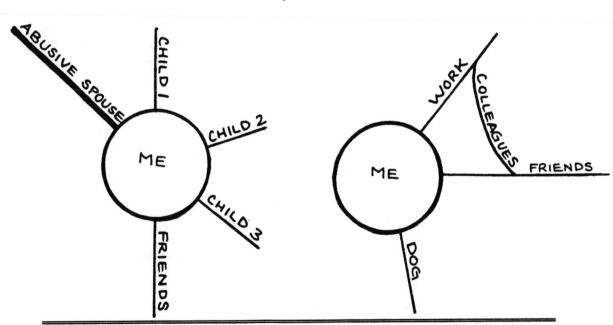

SHOW ME A LIFELINE!
LOOKING AT ONE'S LIFE

Adapted from an exercise by Lorna Cammaert and Carolyn Larsen
Calgary, Canada

OBJECTIVE:
- This exercise, adapted from *A Woman's Choice: A Guide to Decision Making* (1979), constructs a visual representation of an individual's life using significant events from his or her past. It is designed:
  ⇒ to facilitate personal decision making;
  ⇒ to increase understanding of the impact of past events; and
  ⇒ to enhance confidence in future planning.

MATERIALS:
- Paper
- Pencils
- Erasers

TIME REQUIRED:
- Thirty minutes for drawing, plus ten minutes for each participant to describe his or her lifeline

GROUP SIZE:
- Any size

PROCESS:
- Instruct participants to place their paper in a horizontal or landscape position and say, "This exercise is one in which you will draw your lifeline. The vertical axis of your paper represents your feelings about life events, and the horizontal axis represents your age. Choose an age at which you want to start and place your pencil at a point on the left side of your page. Begin to draw your lifeline, depicting how you feel about the major events in your life. Moving your pencil upward will indicate your positive feelings, and moving it downward will show your negative ones. As you move along, be sure that you clearly label the events, and also record, on the horizontal axis, your age when these events occurred."

- Once participants have drawn their lifelines, instruct them to make the following denotations, saying,
  ⇒ "Place an exclamation point ('!') where you took the greatest risk in your life."

⇒ "Mark an 'X' where an obstacle kept you from getting or doing what you wanted."

⇒ "Mark an 'O' where someone else made a critical decision for you."

⇒ "Put a dash ('−') where you made the worst decision of your life."

⇒ "Place a plus sign ('+') where you made the best decision of your life."

- Invite the group to subdivide into dyads or triads to discuss the following questions:

  ⇒ What patterns do you notice about your lifeline?

  ⇒ Are there any surprises?

  ⇒ How have the events you depicted affected your life?

  ⇒ How are your current decisions being affected by past events?

  ⇒ How much control have you had over the events in your life? How much control have other people had in your life?

  ⇒ What events have contributed to your feeling good? To your feeling bad?

  ⇒ What have you learned about yourself from this exercise?

VARIATION:
- Continue the lifeline into the future. Invite group members to trace the events they would like to experience in future.

FACILITATORS' NOTES / TIPS:
- To help you understand this exercise, an example of a lifeline follows on page 134. We recommend that you do not share this example with group members, as it may hinder individual creativity.

***YOUR* NOTES:**

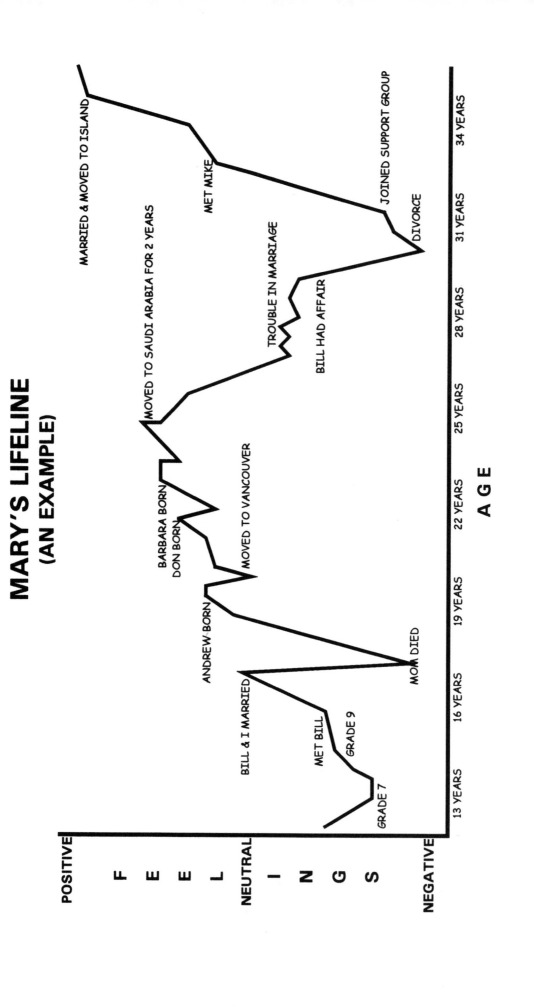

MARY'S LIFELINE
(AN EXAMPLE)

SHOWING YOUR STUFF: EXAMINING COMMUNICATION STYLES

OBJECTIVE:
- To develop participant awareness of verbal and nonverbal communication styles.

MATERIALS:
- Copies of the "Verbal and Nonverbal Communication Styles Worksheet" (see page 136)
- Pencils or pens

TIME REQUIRED:
- Thirty minutes

GROUP SIZE:
- Any size

PROCESS:
- Distribute the worksheets and say, "This exercise will provide you with an opportunity to explore the ways in which you communicate, both verbally and nonverbally.   Answer the questions on the worksheet."

- When participants have filled in their worksheets, direct them to share their responses with two other people.

- After fifteen minutes, reconvene the group and ask members to respond in writing to the following questions:
  - ⇒ What behaviors seem to be working for you?
  - ⇒ What behaviors could be giving people the wrong message?
  - ⇒ What changes in behavior could be to your advantage?

VARIATIONS:
- Tailor the worksheet to your group's purpose (for example, parenting, marriage enrichment, adaptation to a new culture).
- Invite participants to act out the verbal and nonverbal scenarios and videotape the exercise.

FACILITATORS' NOTES / TIPS:
- This exercise is also useful when working with individuals, couples, families, or employees.

SHOWING YOUR STUFF:
VERBAL AND NONVERBAL COMMUNICATION STYLES
WORKSHEET

How do you express your feelings . . .

- when you feel bored with what is happening in a group?

VERBALLY (with words)	NONVERBALLY (without words)

- when you feel annoyed with another person in a group?

VERBALLY (with words)	NONVERBALLY (without words)

- when another person in a group asks you to do something you do not believe you can do well and you feel inadequate?

VERBALLY (with words)	NONVERBALLY (without words)

- when you feel fondness and affection for someone in the group and are uncertain about the feelings of the other?

VERBALLY (with words)	NONVERBALLY (without words)

Chapter 8

Endings

British playwright Francis Quarles wrote this epigram: "The last act crowns the play." This is as true for groups as it is for the theater. Just as the activities at the beginning of a group's existence set the tone for what happens afterward, its final activities act as a positive transition for group members to put into practice what they have learned in the group. Therefore, exercises should continue to be appropriate and carefully planned.

TYPES OF ENDINGS

This chapter presents exercises that are appropriate for three types of group endings: the closure of each group meeting, the final group meeting, and an unexpected departure of a group member.

Closure of Each Group Meeting

Effectively closing each meeting is very important to the group process. Closure includes:

- a summary of the meeting;
- a discussion of homework, such as reading, writing in a journal, and practicing skills;
- plans for the next meeting; and
- encouragement to continue working for positive results.

Depending on the nature of the group, you might consider doing the following:

- encouraging a group handshake or hug;
- offering members a short meditative period;
- reading a short story or poem;
- ensuring group members a safe ride home (especially important for children's groups); and/or
- saying good-bye to each member individually.

The Final Group Meeting

- **Stabilization of Change**

It is important for group members, at this point, to review and summarize, to examine how learning can be transferred to other situations, and to recognize a sense of accomplishment and competence.

- **Celebration**

Ritual endings are a critical part of any group. They are useful for honoring members and acknowledging their accomplishments, and for imparting in them lightheartedness, relaxation, and a sense of completion of a job well done. In celebrating, you might present group members with certificates, scrolls, flowers, candles, group photos, or mementos that befit the purpose of the sessions. When appropriate, spouses, parents, or significant others may be invited to these celebrations.

- **Disengagement**

A group's ending contains elements of denial in which members withdraw their involvement from the group process. This disengagement is essential as people prepare to move on. As the group's facilitator, you must exhibit quiet strength and reassurance, at the same time establishing a lighthearted mood so that participants leave their final session with pleasant memories. Do not, at this point, bring up issues that cannot be solved before the group disbands.

- **Emotional Reactions**

Depending on members' past experiences, the end of a group can evoke feelings of joy or sorrow. Some members may be excited and fulfilled by all they have achieved and anticipate putting their new learning into action. Others may feel sadness, abandonment, and neglect because they are losing a safe haven. Such feelings may engender fear and anger, and you need to be aware that these people may, figuratively speaking, "slam the door" as they leave. Others may not even attend the final session because they "hate to say good-bye." You, the facilitator, may also experience feelings ranging from a sense of loss (particularly if your group has bonded well) to frustration (that the momentum created will now be lost) to relief (at being free of the responsibility inherent in group facilitation).

Unexpected Departure of a Group Member

If you fail to acknowledge the unexpected departure of a group member, you and your group might find "an elephant in your living-room" — feelings of abandonment, neglect, or rejection may interfere with your group's progress. Therefore, it is essential that you address this situation by:

- discussing the effect of the loss on remaining group members;
- conducting a follow-up investigation on the absent member to determine his or her reason for withdrawal; and
- inviting the departing member to a celebration of his or her leaving.

The ultimate goal of this process is to provide assurance that the group and the departing member can flourish without one another.

SELF-EXPLORATION:
LINKING TO THE FUTURE

OBJECTIVE:
- To help members implement their newfound skills beyond the group.

MATERIALS:
- Paper
- Pencils or pens

TIME REQUIRED:
- Five minutes per member

GROUP SIZE:
- Twelve to twenty members

PROCESS:
- Say, "Please write one thing you will do differently because of your participation in this group. Then write about your future plans and aspirations. When you have completed your writing, each of you will share your ideas with the rest of the group."

VARIATIONS:
- After each person speaks, other group members provide positive feedback.
- Seat the group in a circle with a chair in its center. Group members each take turns sharing from this central chair.
- When group members are seated in a circle, a ball toss activity might be used to determine the order in which they share their ideas. The person holding the ball speaks, then throws it to the other person who, after talking, then throws it to someone else.
- Group members may offer to maintain contact with one another beyond the sessions. They might, for example, arrange follow-up meetings, organize a buddy system, or develop a telephone or correspondence system for keeping in touch with one another.

FACILITATORS' NOTES / TIPS:
- Be familiar with community resources relevant to the group, so that you can refer members to them for further assistance.

YOUR NOTES:

THREE WISHES:
ENDING GROUPS POSITIVELY

OBJECTIVE:
- To create a positive ending to a group or to group sessions.

MATERIALS:
- A large candle (refer to the cautions on page 8)
- Matches
- A candle with a protective cuff for each participant
- A table (preferably round) located so that the group is able to form a circle around it
- A dimly lit room

TIME REQUIRED:
- Two to three minutes of quiet reflection time (for participants to consider their wishes)
- Two minutes per member (for them to state their wishes)

GROUP SIZE:
- Ideally, six to eight members; maximum: twenty-five

PROCESS:
- Light the central candle and say, "Choose a candle and form a circle around the table. Think of three wishes:
  ⇒ one wish for yourself;
  ⇒ one wish for the person on your left; and
  ⇒ one wish for the group."

- Now invite participants to take turns coming forward to light their candles from the large one at the center, at the same time expressing their three wishes.

- When all have lighted their candles, read a poem (or direct the group to sing a particular song, or be silent for a few moments), after which group members may bid one another "good-bye."

VARIATION:
- If time is short, request only one of the wishes from participants.

FACILITATORS' NOTES / TIPS:
- This exercise can be used for any special occasions, such as birthdays, retirements, and farewell parties.

SURPRISE BOX:
HAVING FUN WITH ENDINGS

OBJECTIVES:
- To create a lighthearted ending to group sessions, using individual talents and resources and group cooperation.
- To encourage creativity in using a variety of objects.

MATERIALS:
- For each subgroup, a box containing various articles such as clothing, toys, jewelry, books, office supplies, household items, etc.

TIME REQUIRED:
- Fifteen minutes for planning and preparation, plus fifteen minutes per group for setting up and presenting

GROUP SIZE:
- Any size, subdivided into as many smaller groups as time for presentation permits

PROCESS:
- Give each small group a box of objects to be used in creating a skit and then allow them fifteen minutes planning time before they perform.   Remind them that each group member must play a role in the skit.

VARIATIONS:
- Suggest that the skit should relate to the purpose or goals of the group.
- Although chaotic, requiring that subgroups perform skits *without* having time allotted for planning often gives rise to hilarious results. Group members simply gather and someone in the audience shouts out a topic for their skit.   They then look into their box, and use its contents as props to perform *ad lib*.

FACILITATORS' NOTES / TIPS:
- Use this exercise in your group work's middle phase to energize and possibly refocus members on group goals.

YOUR NOTES:

I'M GONNA SIT RIGHT DOWN AND WRITE MYSELF A LETTER: SUMMARIZING ONE'S PROGRESS

OBJECTIVE:
- To remind participants of their own personal growth, as well as gains made in the group.

MATERIALS:
- Pencils or pens
- Writing paper
- Self-addressed, stamped envelopes (provide these, if possible)

TIME REQUIRED:
- Thirty minutes

GROUP SIZE:
- Any size

PROCESS:
- Say, "Write a letter to yourself stating the positive experiences and new insights this group has provided for you. Please be as thorough and specific as you can. When you have finished, place your letter in your self-addressed, stamped envelope, seal it, and give it to me. I'll mail these letters to you approximately one month after these group sessions have ended."

VARIATION:
- Rather than writing a letter, group members might draw a picture or create a poem about their group experience.

FACILITATORS' NOTES / TIPS:
- You must follow through with your promise to mail the letters on the date specified. This is a crucial issue of trust.

YOUR NOTES:

SELF-EXPLORATION:
LEARNING FROM THE PAST

OBJECTIVE:
- To help group members become more aware of their behavior, feelings, and attitudes about terminations.

MATERIALS:
- Paper
- Pencils or pens

TIME REQUIRED:
- Thirty to forty-five minutes

GROUP SIZE:
- Any size, subdivided into groups of five

PROCESS:
- Say, "Write about three group endings you have experienced, for example, leaving school or moving from home.   Think about any difficulties or any successes you've had with them and your feelings toward each of these endings, and describe them on your paper.   When you have done that, write about modifications or improvements that you will undertake as you end your sessions with this group. When you have finished writing, share your thoughts with other members of your subgroup."

VARIATIONS:
- This exercise could be done as a homework assignment to be processed at the following group meeting.
- You might ask each member to share with the rest of the group one positive ending he or she has experienced.

FACILITATORS' NOTES / TIPS:
- Be aware that some participants might dwell on what *didn't* occur or on their own disappointments. You can address this by including the following in your instructions: "If you find that your past experiences of endings have been negative or disappointing, reflect on whether this is a common ending pattern for you.   Then describe the positive outcomes or learning that grew out of your particular disappointing experiences."

***YOUR* NOTES:**

SYMBOLIC REVIEW: MAPPING THE GROUP'S JOURNEY

OBJECTIVE:
- To produce an overall picture summarizing the group's journey.

MATERIALS:
- Flip-chart, blackboard, or overhead projector
- Colored markers or chalk

TIME REQUIRED:
- Thirty to forty-five minutes

GROUP SIZE:
- Any size; however, the exercise is more effective in small groups

PROCESS:
- Say, "This exercise is designed to create a map of the journey our group has taken during the past sessions. Think about the ups and downs and the plateaus we've encountered. What were the highlights, and when did we falter? What were the best and the worst sessions and activities; what are the successes, the disappointments, and the comfort zones; and what are your reasons for these judgments?"

- Ask one group member to begin: "Please tell us what part of the group's journey was especially important to you, and why it was significant, and then perhaps the group will help you to think of a particular symbol (emblem, picture, image, diagram, figure, or letter) that would represent your statement."

- Then ask the participant where on the map he or she would locate the symbol. How high or low would it be? (This may introduce a discussion on whether the map will be linear or circular, and whether choice of color will be significant – if so, will the group want to decide on a particular color arrangement?) Invite the participant to initial the symbol that locates his suggestion.

- Invite the other group members, in turn, to state their ideas on the group's journey, adding symbols and their initials to the map. If one person's idea has already been stated by someone else, direct that person to add his or her initials to the symbol already on the map. Allow the map to grow in whatever creative direction the group takes it. After each group member has had an opportunity for input, invite participants to make additional suggestions of elements to round out the group's journey map.

VARIATIONS:

- After some experimenting as a group to gain understanding of the map's purpose and implementation, invite each member to produce his or her own personal journey map.
- Introduce the "journey map" at the group's first session and update it at subsequent sessions, so that it presents a continuous journal showing the bridges crossed, hills climbed, views enjoyed, and pits encountered.
- Ask group members, jointly or individually, to create a collage of their experiences within the group venture, using photographs, magazine pictures and headlines, and/or scraps of material.

FACILITATORS' NOTES / TIPS:

- It is important to trust that creativity will emerge within your group. Therefore, it is not necessary to be overly directive of the mapping process or to expect a specific outcome.

YOUR NOTES:

GRADUATION DAY: CELEBRATING GROUP ENDINGS

OBJECTIVE:
- To summarize and celebrate accomplishments within the group.

MATERIALS:
- Paper
- Pencils or pens

TIME REQUIRED:
- Thirty minutes planning time plus ten minutes for each group presentation

GROUP SIZE:
- Up to twenty, subdivided into groups of four or five

PROCESS:
- Say, "Create a poem, story, or song that reflects one or more of the accomplishments the group has experienced. Your group will have thirty minutes to plan your ten-minute presentation, which you will then perform for the entire group."

VARIATIONS:
- In a group where a high level of trust has been established, *individual* members might create and perform songs, poems, or stories for the entire group.
- Give members a week to prepare a more thoughtful, in-depth presentation for the larger group.
- Invite outsiders such as parents, spouses, and friends to attend group members' performances of their creations. This provides participants with a bridge back to their family and community support systems.
- Suggest that song tunes may be drawn from nursery rhymes, Christmas music, or popular songs; poems may be limericks or parodies of well-known poems; plays may parody hackneyed plots or feature well-known dramatic characters.

FACILITATORS' NOTES / TIPS:
- This exercise is noted for its flexibility – in time required for preparation and performance, number of performers, and nature of the presentations.

YOUR NOTES:

PARTY TIME: FINISHING IN FUN

OBJECTIVE:
- To give group members an opportunity to create their own celebration, while making use of the knowledge gained within the group.

MATERIALS:
- Paper
- Pencils or pens
- Flip-chart (blackboard, or overhead projector)
- Marker or chalk

TIME REQUIRED:
- Up to one hour for planning

GROUP SIZE:
- Any size.   A large group may require some brainstorming and small group participation.

PROCESS:
- Say, "Let's brainstorm ways in which we can celebrate the end of our group sessions next week. Then we can choose the most popular option and plan for it. In choosing, we should keep in mind that our final decision must be realistic, and it must include all group members."

VARIATION:
- Instead of brainstorming, you might guide the group by suggesting a potluck dinner, picnic, weekend retreat, party, or other celebratory event – which members then plan.

***YOUR* NOTES:**

Chapter 9

Evaluations

This chapter presents evaluative formats for monitoring and assessing interactions in groups. Evaluations are designed to:

- elicit feedback on productive and counterproductive aspects of your group;
- provide information for new directions which will improve delivery of accountable and effective service; and
- teach evaluative skills (e.g., skills in offering constructive feedback).

For a broad range of structured, valid assessment measures, refer to Corcoran & Fischer (1987).

The following questions provide you with guidelines for choosing evaluative formats:

- What is your evaluation objective?
- Are process and/or outcome variables being evaluated? Generally, process evaluation focuses on interactions within the group; whereas, outcome evaluations focus on tasks achieved by individual members or the group as a whole.

- For whom is the information being collected?
- How will the information be used?
- How much time is available to conduct the evaluation?
- When will the evaluation be conducted?
- Who will conduct the evaluation?
- How resistant is your group to evaluation? (A teen group, for example, may consider some evaluative activities boring, unless you use a creative format.)

As a facilitator, you are challenged to deal with the negative feedback you may receive from group members. When this happens:

- Seek clarification whenever possible.
- Strive to maintain an open-minded attitude toward the comments.
- Maintain objectivity. Remember that group members may not be skilled in how to word their comments constructively. Also assess the validity of the feedback in relation to the evaluator's personal biases. (For example, people who rebel against authority may be more critical of your role than others who tend toward submissiveness.) Take responsibility for the changes you can effect, and reject the elements that are beyond your control.

Remember that conducting periodic evaluations alerts you to dissatisfactions before they grow into major problems. This enables you to respond to them appropriately and helpfully.

ALTERNATIVE FORMS OF EVALUATION

Although this chapter focuses primarily on written responses, you might also consider other forms of evaluation.

- **Peer Review**

    Invite a colleague to attend a session and provide you with feedback.

- **Reaction Papers** (Corey & Corey, 1997)

    These are participants' ongoing journals of their experiences within your group. At various phases in your group's development, ask them to respond to questions you choose from the pages which follow.

- **Round Table Discussion**

    Use this method of gathering feedback with caution. Although group members will most often present positive feedback because the norm is to "be nice," negative comments are sometimes voiced. Be aware that these may quickly escalate and create an ending which is deflating. New issues which cannot be effectively handled may emerge from them, causing the session or series to end with "unfinished business." When successful, however, round table discussions are both interesting and useful for participants.

- **Individual Interviews with Participants**

    Use a structured or open-ended format.

EVALUATIVE QUESTIONS

What follows are various questions that can be used to create a customized format to meet the needs of your particular group. A few well-chosen questions will elicit a better response than a long, time-consuming questionnaire. At the end of this chapter there are some creative formats for evaluations. While these have been presented as open-ended questions, they may be changed to closed-ended questions for use with a variety of scales.

Feedback on a Single Session

- What stood out for you from today's session?
- What is the most significant thing you learned today?
- What still confuses you?
- How could the facilitator have used a more interesting approach in this session?
- What could other group members have done to enhance your learning this session?
- What would you like to see happen in our next session?
- What preparation do you need to do for the next session?

Midway Feedback

- Brainstorm a summary of the content of the group, course, or workshop.
- In what way have the goals of the group been met to this point?
- In what way have your personal goals been met to this point?
- What knowledge has been useful to you?
- What do you need to know more about?

- What changes do you suggest regarding preparation and organization of group sessions?
- How is the content of group sessions relevant to your goals and expectations?
- What is the dominant feeling or recurring theme in the group?
- What are the most important values (e.g., respect, fairness, honesty, confidentiality) of the group?
- What particular feelings (e.g., jealousy, sadness) or events (e.g., distractions) may have interfered with group progress?
- What events (e.g., group exercises, discussions, speakers) have helped to move the group forward?
- What comments and suggestions do you have regarding the use of audiovisual aids?
- What would you like to accomplish in subsequent sessions?
- How can the facilitator help you to achieve these goals?
- What can you do to aid your progress?
- How can the group help you progress?

Final Evaluation

Be sure to leave time at the end of your final celebration for group members to consider carefully your evaluative questions.

- How did you find out about this group?
- In what ways have the group sessions met your expectations?
- In what ways have they fallen short of your expectations?
- What specifically did you like about the group? (e.g., group exercises, handouts, homework, small group discussions, guest speakers, lectures)
- Please comment on the length of group sessions, timing, location, physical space, cost.

- What other groups would you like to see offered?   Would you attend?

- What suggestions do you have to improve this group?

- What information have you learned that is relevant to you?

- In what ways did you feel challenged by the sessions?

- Was the selection of group members appropriate to the group's purpose? What changes do you suggest?

- Was the group's size appropriate to its purpose?   How many members do you suggest is optimal?

- What strategies have contributed to effective communication among group members? What alternate strategies do you suggest?

- In what way are you satisfied with the small group discussions? What suggestions might improve these discussions?

- What were the group's major strengths?

- What were the group's major weaknesses?

- Give examples of some of the "fun" things that happened in the group. How might the facilitator incorporate more of these activities into group sessions?

Feedback about the Facilitator

- What general observations do you have about your facilitator?
- Cite specific examples that show your facilitator was well prepared.
- In what ways did your facilitator indicate knowledge and competence in his or her subject area?
- What are your facilitator's major strengths?
- What improvements might he or she make in facilitating a group?
- How was your facilitator effective in involving all group members?
- In what ways was your facilitator supportive, encouraging, and affirming of group members' feelings and ideas?
- In what ways did your facilitator make you feel safe in the group?
- How was your facilitator respectful toward group members and their ideas?
- What methods did your facilitator use to promote creative expression and group member initiative?
- How did your facilitator handle negative situations?
- How was humor used within the group?
- How did your facilitator handle silences in group sessions?
- In what ways was your facilitator helpful in debriefing issues or situations that arose within your group?
- Comment on your facilitator's observation of the agreed starting, stopping, and break times.
- How did your facilitator model risk taking?
- How did your facilitator work toward meeting group objectives?

Feedback about Other Participants

- What progress have you noted in your fellow group members?
- What did you appreciate about your fellow group members (e.g., body language, presentation of ideas, sense of humor)

- How prepared for the sessions were other participants?
- How satisfied are you with the overall quality of other members' participation – for instance, with their preparedness, supportiveness, logic, initiative, sharing, sense of humor?

Self-Evaluation

- How have you grown or changed since joining this group?
- What were you like when you began with the group and how have you progressed?
- What particular skills (e.g., listening, writing, organizing, researching) have you learned in this group?
- What have you learned about how you relate to others?
- In what ways did you have influence on the group and on group decisions?
- Please comment on how committed you felt to the group.
- Please comment on whether you looked forward to the group meetings as something *for you* or as one more obligation.
- How has being part of the group led you to take positive action outside the group?
- In what ways were you made to feel accepted as you are?
- How has the group made you stretch to become better than you thought you could be?
- Write two adjectives that describe how you feel about the group.
- How has what you learned in the group influenced your plans for the future?
- What have you learned about your personal skills and the characteristics that will help you in the future?
- What areas of your personality or character still require some attention?

CREATIVE FORMATS FOR ACQUIRING FEEDBACK

You're in the Movies!

Use a video recorder at various stages in a group's development. Participants usually find this method of following individual or group progress very exciting, but it's advisable that you have their written consent for it. (Prepare a consent form for them to sign.) Also, the technician doing the recording should be someone other than you or a group member. Allow time for showing and discussing the video. If your group has no formal setup, be aware that videotaping can be extremely time consuming.

Stepping onto the Scales

Adapt evaluative questions to a Lickert Scale.

Using a scale of 1 to 5, with 1 being poor and 5 being excellent, answer the following questions:

⇒ How well was this exercise explained to you?   1 2 3 4 5

⇒ Did you have sufficient opportunity to participate in this activity?   1 2 3 4 5

⇒ Did you benefit from participating in this activity?   1 2 3 4 5

⇒ How do you rate the overall value of this exercise?   1 2 3 4 5

Also invite participants to comment on:

⇒ what they liked best about the activity; and

⇒ what suggestions they have for improving the exercise.

Computer Whiz

Computers have ushered in a new way of creating evaluation forms. For the sophisticated computer buff, evaluation forms can take any shape relevant to your group's purpose.

Looking at the Lighter Side: Evaluation Samples

See pages 160 to 165 for examples of evaluation forms that may elicit smiles as well as candid comments about group activities.

Evaluation

What we did well.

What we could do better.

Keep it in!

Leave it out!

Poor   Fair   Satisfactory   Good   Excellent

Anything else you want to tell us?

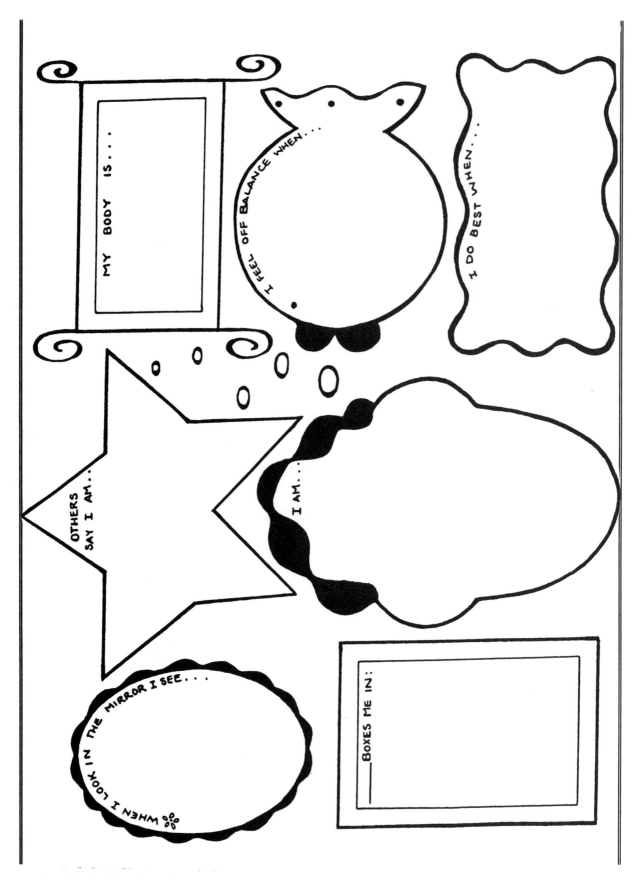

MY BODY IS . . .

I FEEL OFF BALANCE WHEN . . .

I DO BEST WHEN . . .

OTHERS SAY I AM . . .

I AM . . .

WHEN I LOOK IN THE MIRROR I SEE . . .

BOXES ME IN:

Which one describes you?

Evaluation

How do you feel today?

Happy

Worried

Frustrated

Horrified

Anxious

Confused

Calm

Hurt

Sad

Excited

Indifferent

Fearful

Mischievious

Enraged

Curious

Stressed

Guilty

Confident

Angry

Disappointed

GROUP EVALUATION: SUMMING UP

OBJECTIVE:
- To evaluate the broad range of group functioning.

MATERIALS:
- Your choice of questions from pages 153 to 157 photocopied onto individual sheets or written on the flip-chart (blackboard, overhead)
- Paper for recording responses
- Pencils or pens

TIME REQUIRED:
- Twenty to thirty minutes

GROUP SIZE:
- Any size

PROCESS:
- Request group members to complete the evaluation.

- When they have completed it, direct them to divide into subgroups of three to five persons to discuss their responses. Ask each subgroup to choose a spokesperson to present a summary of their discussion to the larger group.

VARIATION:
- Direct participants to record their responses on flip-chart sheets; then tape them to the walls of the room so that other group members may read their comments at their leisure.

FACILITATORS' NOTES / TIPS:
- This evaluation method ensures that all participants engage in the evaluation process and garners more returns than a hand-in or mail-in process.

YOUR NOTES:

A STAR IS BORN!
EVALUATING INDIVIDUAL LEARNING

OBJECTIVE:
- To have group members evaluate what they have learned from the group.

MATERIALS:
- Paper
- Pencils or pens

TIME REQUIRED:
- Twenty to thirty minutes

GROUP SIZE:
- Any size

PROCESS:
- Say, "In the center of the page, draw a circle or star which represents you and print your name in it. Now draw rays from your sun-circle or star. Between these rays, write down what you have gained from your group experience." (see page 169 for a sample format)

VARIATION:
- After participants create their personal suns or stars, direct them to form two equal circles, one within the other. Then say, "The inner circle moves to the right; the outer one moves to the left. When I say, 'Stop,' share your star with whomever you are facing." This can be repeated as time permits.

YOUR NOTES:

A STAR IS BORN!   EXAMPLE

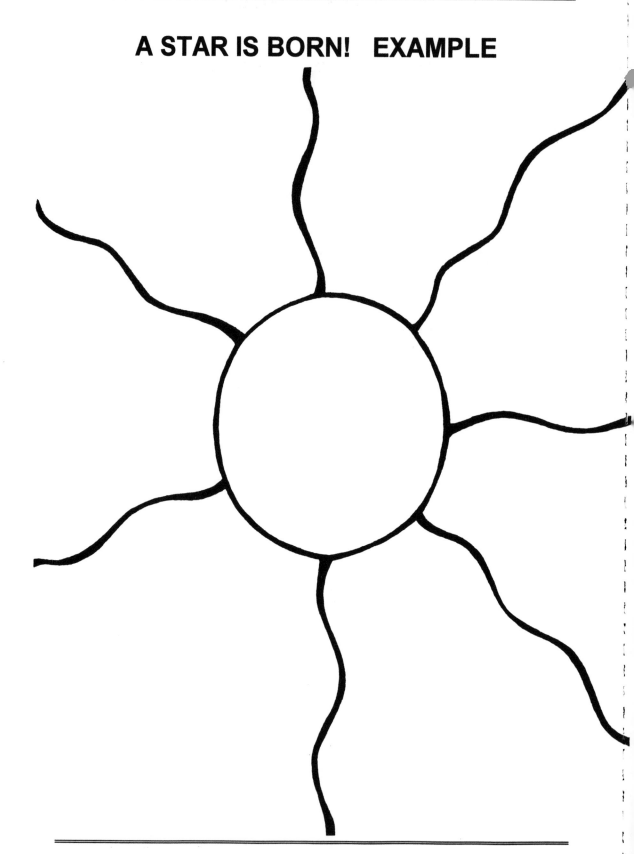

REFERENCES

Arnold, R., Burke, B., James, C., Martin, D., & Thomas, B. (1991). Educating for change. Toronto, Ontario: Between the Lines and the Doris Marshall Institute.

Cammaert, L., & Larsen, C. (1979). A woman's choice: A guide to decision making. Champaign, IL: Research Press.

Capucchione, L. (1979). The creative journal: The art of finding yourself. North Hollywood, CA: New Castle Publishing Co.

Clark, I.J. (1984). Who, me lead a group? San Francisco, CA: Harper Collins.

Corcoran, K., & Fischer, J. (1987). Measures for clinical practice: A sourcebook. New York: The Free Press.

Corey, M.S., & Corey, G. (1997). Groups: Process and practice. Pacific Grove, CA: Brooks/Cole Publishing Co.

Garvin, C.D. (1997). Contemporary group work. Boston: Allyn & Bacon.

Johnson, D.W., & Johnson, F.P. (1997). Joining together: Group theory and group skills. Boston: Allyn & Bacon.

Johnson, I.H., Torres, S.J., Coleman, V.D., & Smith, C.M. (1995). Issues and strategies in leading culturally diverse counseling groups. The Journal for Specialists in Group Work, 20 (3), 143-150.

Reid, K.E. (1991). <u>Social work practice with groups: A clinical perspective</u>. Pacific Grove, CA: Brooks/Cole Publishing Co.

Samuels, S., & Cole, P. (1988). <u>The senior connection: A manual for personal growth and senior peer helping</u>. Ontario: Ministry of Community and Social Services.

Toseland, R., & Rivas, R.F. (1997). <u>An introduction to group work practice</u>. Boston: Allyn & Bacon.

Tuckman, B. (1965). Developmental sequence in small groups. <u>Psychological Bulletin 63</u>, 384-399.

Typpo, M.H., & Hastings, J.M. (1984) <u>An elephant in the living room: A leader's guide for helping children of alcoholics</u>. Minneapolis, MN: CompCare Publishers.

Zastrow, C. (1993). <u>Social work with groups</u>. Chicago: Nelson-Hall.